OVERCOMING THE DESTRUCTIVE INNER VOICE

OVERCOMING THE DESTRUCTIVE INNER VOICE

True Stories of Therapy and Transformation

Robert W. Firestone

 Prometheus Books

59 John Glenn Drive
Amherst, New York 14228

Published 2016 by Prometheus Books

Cover image © Ket4Up/Shutterstock
Cover design by Liz Mills
Cover design © Prometheus Books

Inquiries should be addressed to
Prometheus Books
59 John Glenn Drive • Amherst, New York 14228
VOICE: 716–691–0133 • FAX: 716–691–0137
WWW.PROMETHEUSBOOKS.COM

20 19 18 17 16   5 4 3 2 1

Library of Congress Cataloging-in-Publication Data

Names: Firestone, Robert, author.
Title: Overcoming the destructive inner voice : true stories of therapy and
    transformation / by Robert W. Firestone.
Description: Amherst, New York : Prometheus Books, 2016. |
    Includes bibliographical references and index.
Identifiers: LCCN 2016027672 (print) | LCCN 2016028733 (ebook) |
    ISBN 9781633882515 (paperback) | ISBN 9781633882522 (ebook)
Subjects: | MESH: Mental Disorders—therapy | Psychotherapy | Mentally Ill Persons |
    Physician-Patient Relations | Case Reports
Classification: LCC RC480.5 (print) | LCC RC480.5 (ebook) | NLM WM 400 |
    DDC 616.89/14—dc23
LC record available at https://lccn.loc.gov/2016027672

Printed in the United States of America

*This book is dedicated to my clients, colleagues, and friends
who contributed the truth of their personal experiences
as well as their insights and understanding
to bring this book into being.*

CONTENTS

FOREWORD

Daniel J. Siegel, MD,
author of *Mind: A Journey to the Heart of Being Human*
and executive director of Mindsight Institute

Our minds emerge from both our neural circuitry within our bodies and from the relationships that forge who we are from our earliest days. Our embodied and relational minds are the source of our selves, serving to limit and liberate who we become. When any of a combination of challenges to our minds bombards our development, conflicts may arise that bring great suffering and stifle our sense of freedom and connection.

In this deep dive into the experiences of inner conflict, our visionary guide, Robert Firestone, PhD, offers us wise counsel and fascinating autobiographical accounts of how his important and innovative voice therapy first arose in his own mind, and then how it became a therapeutic practice to help alleviate this "enemy within."

This insightful book offers us a chance to consider how our thoughts are molded by our experiences to either support or challenge our well-being. The psychologist Lev Vygotsky stated long ago that thought is internalized dialogue, meaning we take in our conversations—our communication with others—and shape our own inner voices based on what we've experienced earlier in our lives (1986). Sadly, if such experiences don't go so well, we may have a robust chorus of voices and aspects of our personality, what can be called "self-states," that may create all sorts of havoc in our lives if we don't learn to integrate them well.

Differentiating these voices from each other and from inner

sentiments that are more productive rather than destructive is a crucial starting place for healing. In many ways, this is how we challenge the enemy within as we differentiate and then link these often-demanding and loud voices with a larger sense of the breadth and depth of who we are beyond these often-limiting hostile self-states.

We ignore these inner voices at our own peril. If we believe their absence from consciousness is proof of their absence from our lives, sadly we may be quite mistaken. In this powerful set of stories, you will see firsthand how a master clinician and psychotherapy innovator helps others, and himself, to integrate the mind by freeing the psyche from the prisons of the past.

Research in the field of attachment also reveals that how we are treated by our caregivers directly shapes the function and structure of our brains (Siegel 2012). A fragmented internal sense of self is evident in the dissociation manifest in disorganized attachment (see the range of studies referenced below, including Weinfield et al. 2004). Disorganized attachment can arise with various intensities of terrifying parental behavior, severe abuse, and neglect, which research has demonstrated can lead to impairments in the growth of the integrative fibers of the brain (Teicher 2006, 2007).

In addition, the regulating non-DNA molecules that sit atop our genes—our epigenetic regulators—can be affected by our environment. Fortunately, we are now in a position to scientifically understand that experience, genetic factors, and epigenetic factors lead either to growth or to inhibition of neural connectivity, to either healthy integration or to dysregulated mental life, with the accompanying extremes of the nonintegrated states of chaos and rigidity. Hostile inner voices may be an example of the latter condition: They can be chaotically intrusive and rigidly unyielding.

As you read the pages of this intriguing book, it may be helpful to keep in mind that mental dysfunction—whether it is experientially caused or primarily of genetic origins, or some combination of both—seems to be associated with impediments to neural integration. Healing would mean cultivating integration to create harmony out of a life that used to be filled with chaos or rigidity.

This classic accounting takes us deeply into the challenges to our internal equilibrium. Here you will find in-depth discussions of how to assess the "mindscape" of internal voices and how to help individuals overcome the chaotic and rigid states they can create. You'll be given a feast of stories that can help you both understand and know how to approach hostile inner voices. Such a meticulous accounting of in-depth clinical encounters is not seen much these days, and so this new book about a life's work is a contribution to us all.

The journey we are all on is a lifespan adventure, and it is never too late to find new ways to integrate the many layers of who we are. Soak in the wisdom of our guide's life experiences, and enjoy this fascinating journey of discovery!

ACKNOWLEDGMENTS

I want to express my appreciation to Tamsen Firestone, Jo Barrington, and Susan Short, for their inspirational efforts in editing these stories. I am especially grateful to Joyce Catlett and to Jina Carvalho, communications director of the Glendon Association, who worked closely with Claire Gerus, literary agent, to place this book with our publisher. My appreciation goes to Steven L. Mitchell, editor-in-chief at Prometheus Books, for his encouragement and support of my work, to Jade Zora Scibilia, senior editor, for her insightful suggestions regarding editorial changes, and to Hanna Etu, editorial assistant, for her attention to important details of this project.

Thanks also to the Glendon Association staff, including my daughter Nina Firestone, managing director, and to Megan Fischer, Maureen Sullivan, and Geoff Parr, documentary filmmaker. I want to convey my appreciation to my colleague and daughter, Lisa Firestone, PhD, for her input and ideas in relation to this book, and to my other daughters, Carolyn and Lena Firestone, for their efforts in bringing my work to a wider audience.

I want to express my gratitude to the individuals whose life experiences and personal truths are revealed in this book. I thank them for sharing the insights they gained as they challenged the darker aspects of themselves and gradually grew accustomed to a new and freer way of being and living.

The names, places, and other identifying facts contained herein have been fictionalized, and no similarity to any persons, living or dead, is intended. However, in "Therapist or Tyrant?" and "Afterword: R. D. Laing and the Divided Self," John N. Rosen's and R. D. Laing's real names were specifically retained, but the names of any patients were not.

INTRODUCTION

I began working as a clinical psychologist in the fall of 1957. The moment I opened the door to my first patient, I recognized that the practice of psychotherapy offered meaningful rewards that I'd never dreamed of as a student. Each time I met a client, I'd be fascinated to know this new person who had come to me for help. In the sessions, I'd collaborate with patients in exploring the kinds of thoughts, feelings, fantasies, desires, and dreams of which they may not have been completely aware or had long kept secret. Nowhere in my personal life were people as honest and full of feeling as these men and women were in their sessions with me. Since then, I have lived and breathed psychotherapy. My whole existence from the earliest days of working with severely disturbed patients until now has been devoted to understanding and helping people and to developing myself personally and as a therapist.

Psychotherapy represents a powerful personal interaction and a unique human relationship in which a trained person attempts to render assistance to another person by both suspending and extending him- or herself. Nowhere in life is a person listened to, felt, empathized with, and experienced with such concentrated sharing and emphasis on every aspect of personal communication. When the relationship is characterized by equality, openness, and true compassion, there will be movement toward autonomy and individuation in both parties.

Research has found the therapeutic relationship and the personal qualities of the therapist are among the most significant variables contributing to success in therapy.[1] Above all, the therapist must remain an authentic human being with genuine feelings. Because there is a great deal of controversy within the field regarding which is the most effective therapy and methodology, I feel strongly that the least the therapist can offer the patient is an honest interaction, marked by personal integrity, strength of character, and the moral courage to challenge the status quo. The possibility for the client's growth, ideally, must not be limited by the therapist's defense mechanisms or any tendencies to deny unpleasant truths uncovered in the course of treatment. There is a need to be sensitive to clients' real feelings, qualities, and priorities, and to distinguish them from the negative overlay on their personalities that prevents them from reaching their full potential for living.

The stories I tell in this book are about my personal interactions with real people. They have been fictionalized to disguise the individuals' identities. I've endeavored to portray what actually transpires during therapy sessions, while maintaining strict confidentiality regarding the specific details of each client's story. This refers to any names, places, or descriptive material that would violate clients' privacy regarding their personal lives.

All but two of these psychological tales elucidate key aspects and outcomes of the unique, transformative psychotherapy process. The first exception, titled "Dance of Death," is a powerful account of the underlying psychological factors that led a man to murder his mother. The second, "Afterword: R. D. Laing and the Divided Self," is the story of the death of R. D. Laing, the renowned psychiatrist and literary figure. It is a story of a deep friendship; the brilliant and wonderful man virtually died in my arms.

My main purpose in this writing is to demonstrate the distinctive merits and continuing relevance of psychotherapy in today's world. The short stories and case studies I've chosen reveal the profound impact that self-awareness has on people's lives and their relationships. I believe these personal narratives are worth telling, from both a literary and a psychological perspective. The latter value not only lies in the illumination of the essence of the therapeutic process, but also in the courage shown by anyone who embarks on the arduous expedition toward self-understanding.

MY THEORETICAL APPROACH

Many years ago, I was privileged to work with deeply disturbed schizophrenic patients in a unique residential center. Living with and helping these people come to understand themselves made me acutely conscious of the role psychological defenses play, especially the role of fantasy, in compensating for and adapting to painful emotional trauma. I have spent the remainder of my professional life dedicated to understanding psychological-defense formation, the part that defenses play in people's resistance in psychotherapy and their resistance to pursuing a better life in general.

Neurotic behavior can be viewed as analogous to physical disorders such as allergic reactions or pneumonia. In the latter, the body's defenses to an outside agent are the major cause of the pathology. In the case of mental disorders, the defenses we form are the major cause of our maladaptation later in life.

To the extent that a child is fortunate enough to have parents who are attuned and loving, the child will flourish. To the extent that there is rejection and emotional deprivation, children tend to form a "fantasy bond" with their parents to help cope with the emotional pain they are undergoing. In their imagined connection or union with the parent or parents, children (even adult children) tend to idealize them and simultaneously incorporate, or take into themselves, the parents' critical, negative attitudes. They feel that the parent is good and they themselves are bad or unlovable. This largely unconscious process becomes the "enemy within." The underlying internalized negative thought process, which I call "the critical inner voice," has a very destructive influence on the child's and later the adult's approach to life.

My theory—separation theory—is a synthesis of psychoanalytic and existential theories that explains how defenses formed early in life to protect against psychological pain and trauma are supported and intensified when the child becomes aware of his or her mortality. From that time on, reminders of death support defensive solutions such as inwardness and isolation, alienation, cynicism and distrust, reliance on substance abuse, routines or other escapes, and many other issues. I have found that my theory reflects the core conflict that every individual faces with the awareness of the inevitability of death. The choice is to invest in and pursue love and life, or retreat and attempt to defend oneself; in essence, the option to align oneself with life or to align oneself with death.

HOW I DISCOVERED THE CRITICAL INNER VOICE

The voice was discovered within the context of the therapeutic alliance. The concept of the critical inner voice and the voice-therapy techniques were not directly derived from theoretical considerations; rather they emerged and evolved through interactions between real people.

Early in my clinical practice, I became aware that people appeared to be abnormally sensitive to certain kinds of feedback. For example, many people would become angry and defensive when confronted with information about themselves in group therapy sessions. I also observed that people seemed to prejudge themselves in self-deprecating ways. Therefore, any external commentary or judgment, whether mild or harsh, could trigger self-critical thoughts. I recognized that people are not necessarily hurt by criticisms that are leveled against them—they are, however, overly sensitive when certain criticisms coincide with their own internal self-attacks. In fact, it's not only the truth that hurts. After these early insights, my associates and I began to explore our own self-criticisms and the negative attitudes we held toward ourselves, at a deeper level than before.

Coincidentally, one of my associates, a young woman, was planning to have a baby, but she was aware of feeling lost or removed, both from herself and from others. Once she grasped the idea of giving words to her self-criticisms, she wanted to try out the technique. In a group meeting, she began to recite, in a calm voice, her self-attacks about becoming pregnant. "I'm not fit to be a mother. I don't know the first thing about it. I'll probably mess up."

I suggested that she try to rephrase her self-attacks as if they were coming from an outside person, like, "You're not fit to be a mother. You'll probably mess up." and so on. She started off slowly, repeating, *"You're not fit to be a mother,"* then went on and gained momentum. *"You don't know a damn thing about children. You will be a terrible mother. You're going to screw up your kid! You don't deserve to have a baby."* As she expressed these self-attacks, her face contorted, her speech pattern changed, and she sounded exactly like her mother. This transition seemed eerie to colleagues who knew her mother.

"Just wait until you have children," she went on. *"Just wait until you feel the pain! Then maybe you'll understand what I went through. I just wish the same burden on you. Kids just take, take, take! There's nothing left for you!"*

By this time, the young woman's expressive movements revealed a combination of rage and agonizing sorrow as she exploded with the torrent of emotionally abusive statements toward herself. *"You think you can be a better mother than me! You think you can show me up? That's what this is really about, isn't it? Trying to make me look bad!"*

This powerful release of feeling left her exhausted but relieved. The experience was self-explanatory; there was no need for intellectual interpretation. It was obvious that she had incorporated extremely rejecting attitudes toward herself from her mother.

My colleagues and I were shocked by the intensity with which this young woman expressed her previously suppressed anger. The quality and tone of her self-attacks struck familiar chords in each of us, even though we had not yet verbalized our own self-criticisms in this new format.

What we witnessed that day was an unintentional, yet incredible, "voice therapy" session that would later be duplicated many times by others. The critical inner voice had exposed itself for the first time. We were impressed by the amount of anger directed toward oneself that was brought out by the new technique. All who were present sensed that this was an extraordinary event, and that the new methodology was a discovery of deep significance.

HOW VOICE THERAPY WORKS

In our methodology, voice therapists help the individual to discover and focus on their self-attacks and determine their source. We encourage people to state their self-attacks not as statements in the first person such as: "I am lazy or stubborn" or "I will never get a girlfriend" but as statements in the second person, as though someone was speaking to them. "You are so lazy" or "You will never get a girlfriend." When self-attacks are verbalized in the second format, extremely powerful feelings are released that act as a catharsis. People feel a great sense of relief and intuitively grasp the source of their self-attacks.

Voice attacks are directed toward both oneself and other people. For example, a man calling for a date might think "She will probably never want to go out with you." Or the attack might be directed toward the woman. "She is so superior and snotty, why call her anyway?" Both forms of attack predispose alienation in relationships.

Identifying the source of people's self-destructive thoughts, discovering their origin or causes, challenging them, and answering back all help to alter maladaptive behavior. Later, clients collaborate with the therapist to change behaviors that have acted as obstacles to their goals and were oppositional to their self-development. I refer to this form of therapy as *voice therapy*.

People form different types of attachment patterns of relating to people at an early stage, which is primarily dependent upon how they were treated as children. Generally these patterns persist throughout one's life. People may feel secure in their personal inter-actions with others or feel insecure, anxious, or avoidant, in the way that they relate. The concept of the inner voice described above con-nects directly with attachment theory. Indeed, it is the underlying mechanism at the core of repetitive, maladaptive attachment pat-terns. Internalized voices guide a person's feelings and actions in life. For example, avoidant attachment patterns are controlled by voices that warn people against forming close relationships, "You can't trust people; they will always let you down." or "No one will ever really like you." or "People are no damned good."

The voice must obviously be distinguished from one's con-science, but actually it often predisposes behavior that is contrary to one's values. In fact, it can induce and attack the same behavior. For example, it might encourage you to "just take just one more drink or eat another dessert" and then later turn on you and attack the same behaviors.

It is important to mention that I consider the basic theory underlying voice therapy to be more important than the method-ology, and my therapy approach is not restricted or limited to spe-cialized techniques. The focus is on exposing the negative thought process or enemy within, with an emphasis on feeling. My therapy helps people identify and challenge dependency bonds and destructive "voices," remnants of negative childhood experiences that seriously impair their sense of self, spirit, and individuality.

The stories that follow are characteristic of my therapy approach to individuals in various degrees of emotional distress. They are not simply case histories but are powerful, emotional narratives in their own right that reveal important truths about the human experience. In these tales, I disclose many of my own personal responses as well as my thoughts and feelings during my ses-sions with clients. The therapy relationship is a two-way street because the encounter invariably leaves its mark on both parties. Throughout my career, I have continued to learn from every person I have worked with.

When my clients criticized or exposed negative or hurtful traits in their friends, partners, or family members, I scrutinized myself to look for similar qualities. I attempted to change them. I didn't distance myself from the destructive thinking or alien behaviors of my clients but questioned myself about these matters instead. I thought that this policy made the most of the situation for me. In this unique exchange, I've constantly worked on myself in order to feel better and become a better person.

Shortly before his death, my dear friend and colleague R. D. Laing affectionately put me to the test by saying, "You should take a chance on preaching what you practice." In a sense, that is my aim in sharing these stories. They speak to the triumphs, along with the trials and tribulations, imposed upon the human spirit.

Here, I open the door.

CHAPTER 1

THE UNINVITED

I was a serious twenty-three-year-old graduate student, anxious to complete my education and to get to work in my chosen field. I had started out in a pre-med program, but during my second year at Syracuse University I made the transition to psychology. The decision was fortunate for humanity because I had managed to butcher many frogs and other specimens along the way in my anatomy courses. Ever since making that choice, I had been completely absorbed in everything pertaining to my future as a psychotherapist.

At twenty-three, I already had my master's degree in clinical psychology and was close to getting my PhD. At the time that this story begins, I was part of a study group whose members were feverishly working in final preparation for our comprehensive examinations. We spent all of our daylight hours together, accumulating and reviewing information on virtually every aspect of the field of psychology. Cramming for the test gave our lives a narrow focus, and we existed in a constant state of agitation. After a while, the young men and women surrounding me seemed almost drugged, lethargic from sleepless nights spent studying or just plain worrying. I knew I must have looked the same to them. I joked that the ordeal we clinical psychology students were put through to qualify for our doctorates was likely to cause permanent damage to our psyches and would probably take a toll on our future performance as professionals.

Late one afternoon, I was reading in the small basement apartment that my wife and I shared. I had fallen asleep in my chair when I was awakened by a knock at the door. I thought I heard the voice of an old college friend from Syracuse, Howard Brodsky. I had met Howard several years before; he was a close friend of my roommate and we had all hung out together. I found him likable and fun but had lost track of him when I moved out West.

When I opened the door, I was actually surprised to find that I had been mistaken. Standing there was a member of my study group who had come by to borrow some notes. As I returned to my book, I wondered why I had even thought it could be Brodsky, because I hadn't seen him for over four years. The last I had heard, he was working on a shrimp boat somewhere in the Gulf of Mexico, so there was absolutely no reason to expect him in Denver, Colorado.

One hour later, there was another knock at the door. This time it *was* Brodsky. I had little time to appreciate the amazing coincidence. It took only a quick glimpse of his demeanor to determine that Howard was in serious trouble. I motioned him into our small living room and offered him a seat.

"Howard, what's the matter?" I asked. "Try to talk to me."

There was no reply, just a stony silence. He looked toward me with his big, brown eyes. It was more of a vacant stare than a sign of recognition.

I attempted to establish verbal contact, but my efforts proved futile. I changed my tack.

"Look, Howard, you can stay here for a while, until you feel like talking. You're welcome to camp in our living room. I'll bring in your things from the car."

He sank down into the stuffed sofa and relaxed a little, and I went to empty his car. It was an old Chevy, very messy, filled with all kinds of paraphernalia: an assortment of canned goods, some rumpled-up clothes, various books, a long spear gun, and a high-powered rifle with ammunition. I dumped the goods in the corner of the room, disposed of the ammunition, and came over to where he sat. Holding him by the shoulders and looking straight into his eyes,

I spoke in a kindly voice, "I'm sorry that you're feeling so bad. Take your time here, get some rest, and maybe tomorrow we can talk."

Then I called out to the other room, "Louise, Howard's going to stay here with us for a while. Could you get him some blankets and a pillow?"

Howard became our first houseguest and occupied the living room of our small apartment. Lying in bed late that night, Louise and I pondered his mysterious appearance at our door and my uncanny premonition of his arrival. What could this possibly mean in the larger scheme of things? I wasn't the kind of person who easily believed in extrasensory phenomena and such, but I couldn't help feeling that there was some kind of significance to my precognition. At the very least, it was an odd set of circumstances. More important, we questioned what we were going to do with this strange individual who popped up on our doorstep, and we were worried about Howard's state of mind. I knew that I would have to tackle the situation in the morning.

One thing that I understood was that my friend was hurting. I cared deeply about him and would try everything I could to help. For this reason, Howard ended up staying with us for many months, and he and I talked every day.

During the last phase of preparation for our exams, members of my study group seized on any excuse to let their minds stray from the subject matter. Burt Kahn, a conscientious student with a deep gravelly voice, interrupted my studying, "I hear you have a visitor."

I looked up from my book for a minute, "Yeah, this guy I know just dropped in on me a while back. He was a guy I knew in college, kind of an odd fellow. Actually, he came from my old neighborhood in Brooklyn."

"I hear he's a real basket case," Burt interrupted. It was his compulsive nature to probe.

"Yeah, he really is fucked up," I answered, noticing a slightly defensive tone in my voice. I generally responded like that when I sensed someone was pursuing a line of questioning in an attempt to express disapproval. I knew ahead of time where his questions would lead, and my tone of voice unconsciously reflected it.

"Shouldn't he be in a hospital or something?" he asked, and then he sat back, waiting for an answer. I thought that his prying was probably more a matter of curiosity than anything else, but he seemed argumentative and often exhibited a kind of passive aggression in matters of disagreement.

I closed my book and turned to look at him, "Burt, this guy's a friend of mine and right now he's in a lot of trouble. At this stage, I'm not about to expose him to a typical psychiatric unit. I don't like where that usually ends up. There's no goddamned respect for the patient as a human being, and I don't believe in shock therapy, or even pharmaceutical therapy, except in extreme cases."

I noticed I was becoming angry and tried to be more conciliatory, "For the time being, I'm going to try to help him as a friend, but if I can't, or if things go badly, then I'll have to resort to the hospital alternative."

My companion accepted this explanation but, as always, had the last word. "You're taking on a huge responsibility, Bob. I know I wouldn't want to get involved with this sort of thing. You'd better watch out for yourself."

Before the conversation with Burt, I hadn't thought about Howard Brodsky as a psychiatric patient; he was just a person in distress. Of course, I was aware of my friend's condition; even in those days as a graduate student I could have diagnosed him as potentially schizophrenic, verging on a catatonic state. It just wasn't the way I looked at people, and, for Brodsky, it turned out that my way of sizing up his situation amounted to his salvation.

The day after Howard arrived at my apartment, I woke up early with an uneasy feeling. I leapt out of bed and went into the living room to see how he was getting along. Howard was fast asleep and

I took this as a good sign. At least he was relaxed enough in his present surroundings to get some rest. I went back to bed to catch up on my own sleep before the full day of studying; I planned to talk with him during the afternoon break.

Around noon, I came back home from the university library and found Howard sitting up on the couch in the room exactly where I had left him. Louise mentioned that he had accepted some food for breakfast but had refused to answer her questions. Strangely, his only social response for the first few days was a visible bulge in his pants caused by an erection. No matter who came into the room, whether male or female, his rising member was the only indication that he had taken notice of the visitor. This applied to the dog as well; it was a universal response.

There is a background to the penis story. When Brodsky was a teenager, his penis had been a famous landmark in Brooklyn. Apparently, it was significantly longer and had a greater circumference than most any other. It was described as a veritable salami. Guys came from the far reaches of the borough to catch a glimpse of the phenomenon and would pay good money for the privilege. Brodsky, a shy person by nature, would nevertheless succumb to the financial incentive and permit the viewing. If, for some reason, he felt reluctant, the members of his gang would loudly urge him to comply, and he would eventually submit to the peer pressure.

Association with the fellows in the neighborhood was a mixed blessing for Howard. Due to the crowded and compressed living conditions in Brooklyn, there were large numbers of teenagers in the same age range living on the same block. When a boy or girl's family life was characterized by negligence, cruelty, or derision, the street friends acted as a buffer and functioned as a kind of support group. The kids formed close relationships, had consistent daily contact, and demonstrated strong loyalty. Powerful bonds emerged, and many of the friendships lasted throughout their lives.

But, of course, life on the street was no picnic. The kids were also tough-minded, and their humor could be sadistic at times. It was a hardened, competitive atmosphere mixed with only occasional manifestations of warmth and tenderness.

Brodsky's parents were an odd sort. His mother and father were five foot and five foot two, respectively. Mr. Brodsky was a calculating and extremely aggressive businessman who had achieved remarkable success. He owned numerous buildings in Manhattan, and, in addition to these real-estate interests, he was also in the money-lending business. His mother made a fine living stealing money from his father's pockets. His old man was too miserly to share his wealth even with his own family, so they lived a more or less poverty-stricken lifestyle. This included dressing up in shabby old clothes to apply for charity at the medical center for the needy.

Howard told me another story that further illustrated both how rich and how tight his father was. "One day my father gave me the name and phone number of a girl he wanted to fix me up with. I called her up for a date, and we arranged a time for me to pick her up at her house. The girl's address was far out on Long Island. I drove and drove and finally located the community where she lived, found her street, and pulled up to her door. But it wasn't a door. It was a large gate to an estate, and when I pushed the buzzer and made my presence known, I entered the most beautiful gardens I'd ever seen. When I came up the driveway, I saw several Cadillacs parked there. There were many other obvious indications of significant wealth, including a private dock with a large yacht bobbing alongside it. The house was an amazing two-story residence that looked more like a hotel.

"Well, anyway, I had the date with the girl, who was by no means a beauty, and when I got home, I asked my father how we came to know such rich people. He answered simply, 'Oh, I lend her father money.'"

Brodsky, at five foot eight, towered over his father and was very strong. I remember one day when he was living with us, his parents came to Denver to visit him, and, in a flurry of affection and enthusiasm, he picked up his father and lifted him high above his head. The slight, wiry man was flailing around in the air, arms imploring and feet kicking, shouting, "Howie, put me down! Put me down!" It was a striking scene because of the role reversal. His father, so dominant a personality, and Brodsky, so submissive and acquiescent, had momentarily exchanged positions of power. At the time, I interpreted Brodsky's action as a sign of therapeutic progress.

Brodsky's mother was an intrusive, nagging woman who personified the stereotypical "Jewish mother." During that entire visit to Denver, she never stopped bothering her son for a minute. She was constantly telling him what to do, what not to do, straightening his clothes, fixing his hair, and generally making a nuisance of herself. Brodsky had suffered a hearing loss during the Korean War, but it became selectively exaggerated in the presence of his mother. He would do anything to block out the sound of her voice, and who could blame him?

One incident in particular suggested the insensitive emotional climate in which Howard grew up. As a child, he had a pet rabbit that he was very fond of. His mother was annoyed by the animal because she often found its droppings scattered throughout the house. The rabbit had to be destroyed. His mother's extreme insensitivity and cruelty became evident when, after killing the rabbit, she cooked it for dinner and forced Brodsky to eat it. Brodsky's sister later told me that this sadistic action had a disastrous effect on her brother. She said that his mental problems first manifested themselves soon after that event.

When Brodsky first arrived, I felt patient with my friend and didn't want to pressure him in any way. After a few days, he began to confide in me. He told me about his happy months on the shrimp boat, in spite of the hard physical labor. He had shared a camaraderie with the other fishermen and a love for the sea. Then he spoke of a letter he had received from his father, telling him that he was a no-good bum and that he should come home and be a "mensch" (a responsible and good Jewish boy). The note went on to mention that he was disgracing his family by working as a common laborer. The last lines of the letter had the most-damaging effect: "If you were any good, you would be going to college like the other boys instead of wasting your time. You don't care how this makes us look. I hope you know you are killing your mother."

Howard described how he became confused and felt guilty after reading the letter. His mind was besieged by a tormenting stream of destructive associations and images (strange visions of bloody fight scenes and mangled bodies), and he suffered from periods of intense, undifferentiated rage. He was terror-stricken by his feeling of fury and tried to purge himself from the shame of his hateful thoughts by repeating prayers. Nothing he could do saved him from his inner tumult. His anger kept building; then the destructive voices started. They told him that he was bad and didn't deserve to live. He should just lay low, be still, and avoid people. Finally, he heard voices that commanded him to do away with himself. He said that these injunctions terrified him, and that was why he came to Denver. He had heard that I was studying psychology and hoped I might be able to help him straighten out.

After revealing this information, Howard felt considerable relief and actually managed a smile. I was glad to see that he was safely back among the living and felt confident that I could contribute to his recovery. He gratefully accepted my offer to have ongoing talks with him.

I learned so much from working with Brodsky. It was a confirmation of my earlier experiences with a psychotic woman named Ali and, in particular, my theoretical understanding of schizophrenia. The woman, the wife of a friend, had confided in me about her auditory hallucinations. She felt the sting of imaginary voices that ridiculed her and criticized her every move. She spoke in great detail about how the voices chastised her and suggested punitive methods of hurting herself. I could hardly believe that a person could remain as intact as Ali appeared to be, considering the torture she was enduring. It explained some of the dazed states I had noticed during times when she had acted peculiarly or strangely in a social situation. I had admiration for her capacity to endure without fragmenting from what, to me, would have been insurmountable horror.

I listened intently as she spoke about the details of her hellish existence, and an idea came to me. These hallucinatory voices sounded parental. I became aware that her voices continually admonished her for her "misdeeds." They were similar in tone to the manner in which angry parents chide their children, criticize them or hound them with sarcasm and punitive verbal abuse. The voices she heard were commanding and demeaning as though they came from a superior, or some sort of an authority figure.

I had the thought that these auditory hallucinations were the result of internalized hostile attitudes, stemming from real events in Ali's past—that they somehow split off from her personality and manifested themselves in these disembodied attacks. As I went on listening, I began to take my speculation more seriously. I told Ali about these ideas, and to my surprise, a look of comprehension came across her face. The awful tension was gone and, for the moment, she was very much intact. Over the next months, our conversations brought us closer and Ali maintained significant progress in her personal life. The insight into some of the meaning behind her voices enabled Ali to gain a certain amount of control over them. This fact alone improved her sense of well-being immeasurably.

I began to understand how parental insensitivity, rejection, or hostility are incorporated into the self and become an essential part of the enemy within. This process is known as "identification with the aggressor." Furthermore, in the psychoses there are varying degrees of ego disintegration, a split between the helpless child and the all-powerful parental elements of the personality. This accounted for Howard's dissociative thought processes and tortuous visions.

In the weeks that followed, I continued working with Brodsky.

I helped him realize that the recent onset of his depression coincided with the arrival of the letter from his parents. He had left New York City to escape from an intolerable situation at home and for the first time had begun to value his life. He was leading a simple and independent existence on the shrimp boat when he received the communication from his parents. Basically, the letter attacked Howard's movement toward independence. It was disparaging and intrusive. His parents misinterpreted his quest for freedom as a hostile act toward them. The letter made him furious. He had always felt uncontrollable anger when he caught himself surrendering to his mother's sticky involvement and deceptive manipulation. In this current situation, he panicked when suppressed feelings of rage reached intense proportions that were more appropriate to his childhood.

He could not, as he put it, "give in to the guilt the letter set off and return home," yet he was unable to deal with the turmoil of his mixed emotions. He unconsciously chose the ultimate escape— a retreat into inwardness, a shutdown of all feelings, and a break with reality.

After a few months, as Brodsky gradually began to recover, I asked him to find his own place nearby, and my wife and I reclaimed our living room. He found a studio apartment in a three-story building. It was most easily accessible by a precarious fire escape that hung just outside his window. One morning, I climbed up the fire escape and roused Howard by reaching through the window and gently putting my hands around his throat as a joke. Perhaps I was testing him. Instead of bringing about the anticipated fear reaction, my bogus assault didn't seem to bother him. Howard woke up slowly, smiled sweetly, yawned, and said, "Oh, hi."

For all of his psychological insecurity and fear of people, Brodsky was completely fearless in even the most perilous and calamitous circumstances. He spent countless hours spear-fishing in icy waters in a dangerous area off Brighton Beach, where signs were posted warning of underwater hazards. He would row his small boat far out into the freezing Atlantic Ocean, no matter how large the waves or difficult the conditions.

At a crucial point in our sessions, Brodsky told me about a revealing dream. The content itself was simple and self-explanatory: A robber came into his house and held him up at gunpoint. He was happy to be able to tell the intruder, "I am a lowly bum. I have nothing you want."

Brodsky's associations to the dream all pointed toward the same conclusion: his fear of his competitive feelings caused him to back away and retreat from rivalrous situations. He was safe from an opponent's retaliation only if he never succeeded and did not accumulate any material possessions. It's significant that part of Brodsky's father's vitriolic attack in the letter defined Howard as a bum. I conjectured that his father was insecure as a man and had been threatened by the birth of his son. That was why he continually demeaned Howard and belittled his achievements, why he took advantage of every opportunity to assert his superiority. The boy, the victim of this unrelenting assault, had been besieged by feelings of inadequacy and worthlessness all of his young life.

On an existential level, the robber in his dream symbolized his father's competitive attack that "robbed" him of his life and vitality. But Brodsky had a solution: if he had no success, if he had no life, he had no vulnerability. Being the lowest of the low was his primary defense. He turned each defeat and blow to his self-esteem into a perverse triumph in an attempt to switch his father's attacks into a personal victory. He took refuge in his masochism, accepted the miserable identity that was thrust upon him, and found a false sense of safety. In matters of life and death, Brodsky felt he had nothing to lose.

At last summer arrived. I had passed the comprehensive exams with high marks and was preparing to leave Denver for my work with Dr. John Rosen, the founder of Direct Analysis. But what was I to do about Brodsky, who still needed follow-up therapy? The obvious solution was to send him to my own therapist, Dr. Mazer, for treatment during my absence. In my last session before my departure, I brought up the matter and he agreed to take Brodsky on. The issue was settled and I wished Howard continuing success.

When I returned to Denver from Rosen's for my final year of grad school, I renewed my friendship with Howard. Life for me and my associates at the hospital consisted of hard work by day and all-out partying by night. During the entire month of December, incredible celebrations were attended by virtually every mental-health professional in the city. They consumed huge amounts of alcohol, and I, who drank very little, wondered about the quality of treatment the mentally ill received in the city of Denver during the Christmas season. Over the course of an evening, some people would pass out on the floor or couch, and Brodsky would carry their limp bodies to one of the bedrooms and pile them on the bed to sleep it off. He wasn't all too careful and would occasionally bang heads and limbs against the walls and doorways.

I had an awkward exchange with Dr. Mazer regarding Brodsky. Pondering Howard's therapeutic situation, I considered that I was the better person to treat him and when I offered my services, Howard decided to come back to me. Dr. Mazer was annoyed at the cocky manner in which I spoke to him about the transfer, and he made the comment, "The Lord giveth and the Lord taketh away." I realized that he was absolutely right in his attack on me, and I accepted the fact that I had behaved in a superior and condescending manner. I still thought that my assessment was valid, but I had learned a valuable lesson about vanity. After all, I was still a student and he was an experienced psychiatrist.

Time passed, our working together went well, and eventually Brodsky went off to Israel, where he met his future wife. Shortly thereafter I heard that he had moved back to New York. Twenty years later, I was passing through the city and called Brodsky to say hello. I learned that he had two grown sons. He informed me that he had his own business going, but he was quick to add, "Don't get the wrong idea, I'm not that financially successful or anything."

CHAPTER 2

DEMON ON MY SHOULDER

Several years later, in the early 1970s, a psychotherapist who was an acquaintance of mine came to me in a nervous, frightened state. When I ushered Dr. Stanley Levin into my office, I felt pained as I witnessed his obvious discomfort. I asked him what was wrong, and he immediately began to describe his concern about his sessions with a client named Paul Berger. He diagnosed the man as suffering from extreme paranoia and rage. Levin also told me that he was worried that Paul was becoming dangerous; in fact, Paul had actually threatened to kill him!

Stanley had first seen Paul as a teenager in family therapy. He told me that Paul was one of the strangest individuals he'd ever met and that Paul's parents were probably two of the most rejecting individuals he'd ever worked with. Some years later, he had begun working separately with Paul as a private client. The sessions went fine for a time, but after a while the situation had deteriorated and their interaction was becoming increasingly alarming.

I couldn't help asking, "Why did you come to me about this?"

"Well, first I thought that you would understand this type of client because of your past experience with psychotic patients. Second, and more important, I wanted to ask if I could refer him to you."

"Thanks a lot," I said jokingly, but I immediately added that I would be willing to look into the matter. I followed up by offering to meet with Mr. Berger the next week.

Stanley looked relieved and appreciative. When he left, I couldn't help but question why I'd made the offer to meet his client. After all, my practice was busy and my life was uncomplicated, so I seriously wondered about my willingness to enter into such a tense, potentially dangerous situation. Was I looking for trouble? Or did I just enjoy the challenge?

The next day I received a phone call from Paul Berger, asking for an appointment. I arranged to see him the following Tuesday afternoon at four o'clock. Over the weekend, I thought about the upcoming encounter, wondering what the interview would be like. I told myself to let it go and to enjoy what I was involved in at the moment, but I was not always successful.

On Tuesday afternoon, Mr. Berger arrived exactly at the appointed time. He was about five foot nine, with a medium build, and although he was exceptionally polite, his facial features betrayed deep anger. In fact, he had the look of a Scrooge; yet, sometimes his face had the appearance of an innocent, naïve child. He spoke in words that painted vivid pictures for me, but his personal communications were sometimes hopelessly tangled.

Indeed, it was often difficult to determine if Paul's words or emotions came out the way he intended. On one level, he spoke and thought logically and coherently; on another, he had bizarre, irrational thoughts. He manifested positive attitudes of reaching out to others, but his views of himself and others were extremely hostile and cynical, making his presence difficult to tolerate.

Overall, there was something childlike and inconsistent about his demeanor. When he spoke, his eyes would often tear up, revealing his underlying sadness. He was an enigma, a mixture of two people, a fragmented personality: one side was angry, even rageful; the other, soft and emotional. It was the former that had caused Stanley to fear him.

Considering the buildup to our first encounter, I was surprised that I felt comfortable with Paul during our first meeting. In some basic way, I could feel the sensitivity and hurt beneath his gruff exterior. I also appreciated the fact that he was highly intelligent.

As Levin had noted, Paul's disturbance consisted of a well-developed system of paranoia, an orientation of deep distrust and cynicism toward others that was extremely difficult to confront. His negative expectations created real problems in relationships and became a self-fulfilling prophecy. He mentioned that his irrational fears also extended to imagining impending assaults by strangers. For example, he felt uncomfortable and would avoid walking past a group of adolescent boys because he feared they might physically attack him.

I knew that at some point I would have to directly confront his paranoid orientation and would eventually have to cope with any hostility being directed toward me. That was the task that I had anticipated when I took on the referral. Nevertheless, I felt I could help Paul, and at the end of the intake interview, I told him that I would accept him as my client but would like to get some ground rules straightened out first.

I spoke in a somewhat-stern, angry tone, "What have you been trying to do, scare people?"

Paul mumbled something, but I just went on admonishing him. "I don't deal with crazy people. I only talk with people who want to help themselves—not crazy people." I continued passionately, "Never scare my associate again—not him or anyone else—with any crazy talk or behaviors." This was my way of setting limits.

Paul said, "I get what you're saying and I know that I can control myself." He thanked me and looked genuinely appreciative.

I believed him but reinforced the fact that he could, indeed, control his emotions. I explained that it was completely acceptable to freely express his feelings during our sessions but stressed that that was where it ended. Again, I strongly emphasized that he must take absolute control over his destructive actions. We talked for a while longer, and then I set up our next appointment for the following Tuesday.

One of the reasons Paul had sought therapy was because he and his wife had been thinking about having a baby, but the thought actually filled him with dread. The couple had no close friends, and he was deeply concerned about the negative effect that his social ineptness and isolation would have on a child. He explained that his rigidity and lack of warmth typically caused people to avoid him or dislike him, and he feared these would have an impact on him and his children, should he become a parent.

Paul complained strenuously about having no memory of his childhood prior to adolescence and said that he hoped to recover these memories through therapy. But the most immediate, compelling reason Paul had finally decided to seek professional help was the onset of recent events that had precipitated a crisis of serious proportions.

He began by describing the prevailing situation before the trouble started. "I got involved with my first wife, Gloria, in high school. We were sexual a lot and she got pregnant almost immediately. When the baby was born, she put it up for adoption. We'd never considered keeping the kid, and even then, I must have felt that I would be destructive to a child. We got married after graduation and settled in Honolulu, where we lived for several years, more or less happy."

Paul continued, "The only strange thing about those days was that I knew that I had some, let's say, *odd* sexual habits."

"What do you mean by that?" I probed, curious about the direction this session was taking.

He looked awkward and stammered out. "Like I . . . uh, uh . . . I would look for a lot of diversions to keep up my excitement."

"What would you do?" . . .

"Well, I liked to put objects in her vagina, like a banana or cucumber. One day I put a large cucumber in her and we went out walking to a movie and it excited me. Does that make me some sort of pervert or something?"

I thought a moment, knowing I had to quell my instinctive response and respond with detachment. "Well, I think we have to look into that sort of thing to see what it means to you; that's the important element here."

"I see what you mean," he agreed, and we agreed to pursue the matter in future sessions. Then, Paul said there was something even more pressing that he wanted to talk about. "One summer when my parents and brother visited us, my brother and I had a horrible argument, and I felt worse than I ever had in my life. I told Gloria that I wanted to go back to the mainland. I even used my phobia about bugs and mosquitoes as a reason to leave. Looking back, the truth was that I felt such a terrible, empty feeling from their visit, I believed I could never be happy there again. I thought that by leaving Hawaii, I might manage to feel a little bit better.

"Now I can see how fragile I was at the time. I literally rewrote history from having a dream job where I was liked and appreciated, living pretty happily in a perfect location in Hawaii, having a fun relationship with my wife, to—in one afternoon—hating my work, believing the heat was insufferable, hating the bugs, finding my work associates boring, catching island fever (which I'd had never had until then) and being compelled to find another place—any place—to live, and quickly!"

"What a turnabout!" I reflected, happy to see him gradually opening up.

"It was definitely harebrained and crazy. To have spent one miserable week with my parents and brother, and then to rewrite everything in my mind, to change a perfectly good life into one so bad, I had to get away as quickly as possible. That can only be called 'crazy.' But that's what I did."

"I don't know that it was crazy, but seeing your parents was obviously immensely stressful. It really shook you up. What actually caused your extreme reaction? What crossed your mind?"

"I guess it reminded me of my childhood in some way, when I always felt rejected, stirring up old feelings that I felt as a kid. To be truthful, I think that deep down, I really hated all of them."

"You hated all of them, probably for good reasons, but you took it out on yourself, throwing away your whole life."

"I guess I must have felt pretty guilty. . . . You know, I just thought of a strange thing." He paused. "When I told Levin about hating my parents because I felt they never loved me and only cared about my brother, he said that they really must have loved me, but just had a hard time trying to show it."

He looked up at me. "That's what pissed me off so much toward Levin. He was full of shit, and it messed up my reality."

"I can totally understand your reaction," I agreed. "That would make anybody mad, and Levin's response fed right into your own guilt feelings." I recognized that Levin had made a significant therapeutic error in his response to Paul.

"Wow, this stuff is beginning to make sense. Thanks!" Paul said, sighing deeply. He continued, "After we moved from Hawaii, Gloria and I eventually came back to Los Angeles and I found a job. A few months later, I started to imagine that I was about to be fired. Thinking that my boss was getting rid of me, I quit and went back to school, taking business and accounting courses."

"Why did you think you were about to be fired?"

"I felt like my boss had it in for me," Paul said vaguely. Then, he remembered a different incident that supported his paranoia. "It's a long story, but eventually I started my own business and met Lorraine. She was pretty, and I was completely knocked out by her. She was small, had a really cute figure, and was smart and spunky. Dating Lorraine was an exciting and mostly happy time for me. The trouble was that I felt guilty cheating on Gloria, but in time I separated from her and later, we were divorced. Shortly after that, Lorraine's father came to the store where she was working. He knew I would be waiting to pick her up, and he was furious. He chased me around the parking lot, raising his fists and threatening to kill me if I didn't leave his precious daughter alone. I was terrified. It was very frightening and also guilt-provoking. It really fit in with my fear and distrust of men. You can see why I need therapy!"

After getting familiar with these preliminary details and beginning to gain Paul's trust, I felt that it was time to settle down to working on the core issues that troubled him.

My general therapeutic approach involved traditional psycho-analysis, but I also utilized a deep feeling methodology along with my own technique, which I termed "voice therapy." Traditional psychoanalysis sometimes involved deep breathing and letting out sounds that often culminated in a release of powerful emotions and a flood of insights connecting past trauma and current events. Voice therapy involved speaking—verbalizing attacks and hostile attitudes toward the self and others in a dialogue format. The result made it appear as though these comments were coming from someone else.

For example, instead of saying, "I'm stubborn" or "I'm bad," a person would say it as a "voice," as though someone else were talking to them: "*You're* stubborn" or "*You're* bad." By framing them as external "voices," people could separate themselves from their attacks on themselves and others, and then identify their source. Later, they would learn to answer back both emotionally and rationally.

I felt that this voice-dialogue technique would be of great value to Paul because he was so troubled—mean toward himself and malicious toward others.

As I got to know him, I learned that Paul had a continuous "tape" playing in his head that degraded everything. He once described this process as, "... it's like a demon sits on my shoulder and continually ridicules me."

I asked him to express the "demon" as a voice. He found it easy to adopt the technique and entered into the dialogue:

"*You little creep, you're too stupid to do a good job at work. Sooner or later, you're going to make a terrible mistake; then all your fancy ideas of success will come crashing down on your head. And you'll deserve everything you get, you miserable shit!*"

Paul's voice attacks approached the level of an external source by interrupting and almost drowning out his rational thoughts.

Early in therapy, Paul's hostility and paranoia focused on his distrust of me. In the course of treatment, he developed strong negative-transference feelings from the past, based on feelings of hostility and distrust in relation to his father. Although he had sought my help and trusted me to a certain extent, on another level he was deeply cynical, and his behavior was unpleasant and provocative during our sessions.

Paul's resistance in therapy took the form of guarded, vague ramblings and a seeming unwillingness and fear to make his attacks on me directly. Instead, he tended to blurt out angry questions, "Why are you looking at me like that?" or "What did you mean by that last statement?"

Eventually, he learned to put his suspicions and hostile thoughts about both me and our work into voices: *"Look, you idiot, this man is going to influence you in the wrong direction. He's going to sit you down and brainwash you and you'll have no opinions of your own after he's through with you. You can't trust him. You'd better listen to me, Paulie, if you know what's good for you. You were always a gullible, stupid kid."*

The meanness of these attacks ate away at Paul's confidence in me; he began to act superior and authoritarian to compensate for his feelings of worthlessness. His attacks on others were just as intense. For example, Paul told me about one evening when he was driving a few friends to a movie. He was in a rush to make the 8:00 p.m. show, and he had to stop for a pedestrian in the crosswalk. As he waited for an old man with a metal walker who was painstakingly making his way across the street, Paul was muttering, "Good-for-nothing bastard! I bet that metal contraption is fake. He's not handicapped. He's just walking slowly to fuck me up. He's going to make us all miss the movie. I'd like to run him over!"

He reported that the people in the car were shocked, but for Paul, this was a typical reaction. His response to frustration amounted to the ravings of a lunatic. Over time, I became better acquainted with this dark side of his personality.

During his sessions, Paul continued to be hostile and demanding. When I restated his accounts of his parents' neglect and abuse, he defended them as being basically good people. This directly contradicted what Dr. Levin had relayed to me. Levin had said that in addition to rejecting Paul outright, they clearly preferred his brother, Luke, and made no effort to conceal it.

Paul's ambivalence and denial of his family's shortcomings led him to develop a split view that presented them as good and himself as "bad, dirty, and disgusting." At the same time, he tried to compensate for this negative self-image with vanity and feelings of superiority toward others.

When he was finally able to express his paranoid thoughts toward me as voice attacks, they ran down my character and qualifications as a therapist: *"This man is out to get your money. What does he know about people? You think he's read all these books on his shelves? For all you know, he's a quack, a fake. If he's so darn good, why isn't he more well-known?"*

Paul identified these as sounding very much like his father's point of view. When I was about to leave for a three-week vacation, he became fearful of the idea of me being gone for a prolonged time. His fear was compounded by the fact that he was planning to undergo a minor surgery during my absence. In our last session before my vacation, Paul verbalized this fear of separation in the form of a voice: *"See, now you're hooked. What are you going to do now? What right does he have to go away?"*

As Paul spoke, he looked sad and started to tear up.

"He's always been around, so now he's going to go away. He knows you're going to have that operation; that's just when you need him. What does he mean, 'You're just scared?' Of course, you're scared, you need somebody to take care of you. That's what you're paying him for, isn't it?"

Despite his resistance, after approximately a year of therapy, Paul began to develop positive feelings that challenged his paranoid distortions; slowly, a softer, more vulnerable side of him began to emerge. Both he and I thought it would be valuable at this juncture to confront his characteristic lack of generosity. So together we discussed a number of possible corrective suggestions in the form of extra bonuses to his employees and simple acts of generosity toward his friends. Initially, Paul was afraid and reported a number of voices telling him that he was a fool, *"You're an idiot, a pushover. They'll just take advantage of you."* But he eventually accepted the suggestion.

When Paul first started his own business, his cynical, judgmental voices about other people were expressed in belittling, sarcastic one-liners aimed at his employees. He noticed that by berating others at the office, he was sometimes able to relieve the voice attacks toward himself, but on the other hand, he hated himself for mistreating them. As Paul slowly and painstakingly isolated his distorted attitudes toward other people and controlled his tendency to verbally abuse his employees, he began to break down his fundamental resistance to changing deep-seated character defenses of suspicion and cynicism, and his ungenerous nature.

In one session, Paul began to deal with these issues. "My business is growing fast, so I guess it's time to start being more generous with the money. I'm planning to share what I can with my partners and employees. This is no stupid fantasy, and not just because of your suggestions," he asserted, looking at me briefly. "It's a real desire and I am already financially successful enough to do it. My negative side seems to be taking a rest! Of course, my nasty demon gets me sometimes when I'm alone, but it doesn't matter very much. I've already made my decision to share my business success with others."

Later, he found that generous actions gave him pleasure and led to friendly responses from people. He discovered that these acts of kindness, surprisingly enough, helped dispel his deep-seated fear of being exploited. Paul once reported this period as being the "happiest time in my life."

The fact that people responded favorably to his generosity, as they often do to people who implement positive suggestions, moved Paul beyond the limitations he had previously imposed on himself. He did have to adjust to the feelings of closeness and increased vulnerability brought about by these unfamiliar positive experiences. He then had to cope with the anxiety aroused by the disturbance of his previous psychological equilibrium.

Verbalizing any nasty thoughts that arose, understanding their source, and answering back relieved a lot of Paul's anxieties, and he went on to form valuable insights. As he progressed in these talks with me, I suggested that he join one of my therapy groups, which he did. Gradually, Paul began to show improvement and slowly, after much testing behavior, he became a likable person. Interacting with the other group members who shared a compassionate understanding of his dark side, Paul began to choose again and again his "good" side. He progressed well and eventually terminated therapy. However, this was not the end of my story with Paul.

A couple of years later, Lorraine left Paul. That precipitated another crisis in his life. Her departure was a particularly traumatic experience for him because he had always had a deep fear of being abandoned by a woman. Now, Paul felt alone, in turmoil, and desperate when he asked to return to therapy. I agreed to take him on and encouraged him to maintain a journal of what he was experiencing to help him recover relevant memories of his early childhood. He wrote:

> It was Saturday morning when Lorraine moved out of our apartment in the Marina. Right away I called you to talk about my plans. I was deeply shaken even though I had had the feeling for a few weeks that she might leave at any time. We hadn't been getting along very well for a long time. I had simply been blocking out that knowledge with my intense preoccupation with work. Now it's over. Lorraine is gone and this damn apartment is empty. It's filled with beautiful furnishings, but it feels so dead to me. It suddenly struck me that I don't want to be alone the rest of my life, driving women away and making enemies everywhere I go. My heart was pounding and I felt as if I could hardly breathe as I pulled into your parking lot. I was determined to be clear about what I wanted to do. Funny, I didn't feel confused in

the least, and I had confidence that my words wouldn't come out garbled the way they usually had.

Paul looked pale and disheveled when he entered my office. Once he was seated, words and feelings spilled out. "I want more than anything else in the world to become the kind of person who can have friends. I feel sick of pushing everyone away who means anything to me. I admit that when Lorraine first left me, I was insanely angry at her and had feelings of wanting to get even with her or hurt her in some way. But I knew I could control those feelings, that I wouldn't act on them."

"I commend you on your control," I offered, meaning it.

"In the middle of talking about Lorraine just now, I suddenly had an image of my mother standing at the back door of our house, looking at me with a really mean face."

I asked him to free-associate about this image, that is, to say all his thoughts as they occurred to him without censoring anything, if possible.

"I see other images. It's like a series of pictures, popping up in my mind. Now everything feels like it's falling into place. I have this clear memory of something that happened when I was barely six years old. I was riding my bicycle down a steep hill and it went out of control. I rode straight into a moving car, flew over the car onto the grass beyond . . . and I got hurt. The driver got out of the car and wanted to see if I was hurt, and to try and make me feel better. I was angry at him and I picked up my bike and started to stomp home as he called for an ambulance. The ambulance came, but they couldn't stop me either.

"Finally, I got to the back door of my house and banged on the door. It was a locked screen door and my mother wouldn't respond to me because I was crying. Finally, she said, 'Stop crying and I'll let you in.' And I kept crying and trying to get her to open the door. She repeated her ultimatum over and over. Finally, the ambulance driver broke the door down. The car driver and the ambulance guys were pissed at my mother for not letting me into the house. Also, they were furious at her for letting me ride my bike in that neighborhood and on that hill, particularly because it was so steep and led to cross traffic in front of an elementary school. There was no way to control a bike on it. I know I would never think of letting a child ride a bike alone in that area, let alone down that hill!"

"Basically, you're saying that she had no feeling for you," I suggested.

"Shit, worse than that, I think that she *wanted* something bad to happen to me."

As Paul developed more insight into the neglect he had experienced in his family, he began to see his parents more objectively. Subsequently, his tendency to "listen" to or believe his voice attacks diminished significantly, and he began to feel better.

Around this time, he became caught up in plans to fly with three of his friends to Alaska in a private plane. Paul had never before traveled in an adventurous, spontaneous style. His vacations with Lorraine had always been carefully scheduled luxury cruises. Now he was going to rough it. While Paul was enjoying the flight over the vast expanses of Canada and Alaska, he was also seriously working on his own "therapy." On the trip he diligently wrote in his journal.

> I was determined to overcome the long-standing phobia I had of bugs, flies, mosquitoes—any small creature like this scared the wits out of me and made my life miserable whenever I was outdoors. One day, we went to a lake where there were thousands of flying bugs and mosquitoes swarming in the woods. Ordinarily I would have stayed in the car. Instead, I stood out there in the middle of a grove of tall pine trees and let the bugs swarm around me. I forced myself to stay there for a half hour. I was shaking; perspiration was dripping from every part of my body and covered my clothes. There was a hard lump in my stomach and I felt revulsion rising in my throat. I was determined not to throw up or run for the car. After a time, some of the worst

symptoms went away and I felt comfortable walking around the picnic area. Since then, I haven't panicked over bugs. I'd say that I successfully desensitized myself.

Paul also wrote about another subject that had troubled him:

Dr. Firestone and I often talked about my travels in my sessions. I had this fascination with far-away places—the farther the better, it seemed. Zermatt, England, Japan, Tahiti, France, Greece, Israel, Egypt were all places Lorraine and I had visited. For months preceding the actual travel, I'd be focused on the visual side of the places—as if I were there enjoying the wonders of those places already. As if I were in a dream. When I finally arrived at these exotic places, my feeling was that here was a place that was bigger (visually, aesthetically, physically) than my troubles . . . and I felt at peace with myself. Quieted. Calm.

Dr. Firestone's interpretation was that I was using the obsessive planning and the fantasy world I created around travel to run away from my feelings—just as I had when I was a child, running away from home (from being neglected by my parents), and that the places I went were, in fact, bigger than the voices I heard in my head—the parental voices that accompanied me everywhere—and that I was trying to drown them out by travel. Made sense to me! Since then, although I still love to travel, I always question whether I'm running away from something or really desirous of going to that place. Certainly, the addictive aspects are gone.

Another goal of mine in seeing Dr. Firestone again was that I didn't want to continue to tear him down as I had before. I began to trust him much more and became interested in his life, his ideas and his experiences. He didn't say that much about himself, but my trust and interest in him enabled me to look beyond my own fixed view of things and listen to his take on different issues. It widened my consciousness—trusting his opinions. Soon I branched out and trusted other people as well.

Paul once again participated in group therapy, which helped him overcome his strange attitudes toward people, particularly women and sex. In these sessions, Paul listened as men and women revealed their sexual fantasies, fears, and inadequacies. He learned that it was okay to say anything he was thinking on this subject, no matter how peculiar or bizarre.

More important, he came to understand that his inserting cucumbers and other objects into his girlfriend was part of a sadistic reaction to women based on his hatred of his mother. Ridiculing and humiliating his girlfriend was an indirect way of getting even for the original pain that his mother had caused him. As he exposed his negative views of women and sexuality and developed insight into them, he began to experience a major change.

Paul still spoke in a way that people sometimes had trouble following—his leaps from one train of thought to another were made without a logical bridge of association, but people in the group listened attentively anyway. At times, his manner of speaking became a source of amusement for himself and his new friends. He came to enjoy others' good-natured teasing about his eccentricities. He even began to make jokes about himself. His developing sense of humor acted as a strong antidote to his profoundly serious, accusatory demon. Paul learned to laugh at his faults and weaknesses, whereas before he had sneered at himself derisively.

The women Paul dated after his separation from Lorraine were sensitive and friendly. Meghan was one woman Paul particularly liked; she had a more open outlook about sex than Paul was used to. She helped him get over the remnants of his most critical feelings toward women. For example, Paul was offended by a woman's "smell" during sex and he intensely disliked "wet French kisses." With humor and a great deal of patience, Meghan helped Paul work through his fastidiousness in relation to sex. She had an understanding of his idiosyncrasies, and her saving grace was her sense of humor. Without her ability to laugh off Paul's sarcastic one-liners and criticisms, this relationship would never have lasted. Damaged herself by a harsh upbringing, Meghan was a real friend to Paul because she felt compassion for the ways he had been hurt.

Eventually, they married, and they have maintained their relationship for more than twenty years. In so many ways, Paul has triumphed over the demon. Once somewhat of a dangerous fiend, nowadays, Paul has become a kinder, gentler soul.

It required several years of psychotherapy for Paul to completely separate out his paranoid distortions from his more-rational ways of thinking. Interestingly enough, throughout both phases of his therapy, Paul was able to recover only fragments of memories of his childhood. Nevertheless, he succeeded in uncovering the hostile, cynical thoughts underlying his overall maladjustment, as well as his fears of being close to a woman. The therapeutic process enabled him to rebuild his trust in other people and in himself.

CHAPTER 3

THEY SENT HER HOME TO DIE

They sent her home to die because there was nothing more that the hospital could do for her, and death was imminent. Lena was eleven years old, had serious asthmatic symptoms, and had been sent to the hospital for special care. It was a research institution in Phoenix that took only the most serious cases of asthma. The typical treatment results of this facility attested to the remarkable achievement on the part of hospital and staff. It was because of a unique and powerful psychological approach that the facility achieved widespread success in reversing prognoses that were initially seemingly hopeless.

An essential part of the cure was to separate the children from their parents for a two-year period. During this time, only two brief visits with loved ones were permitted. Despite the loneliness and hardship of the drastic separation, many of the children's asthma symptoms improved immediately with the break in contact with their families.

The children ranged in age from five to sixteen and had to have been diagnosed by their physicians as suffering from severe, intractable asthma. Prior to the time of admission to the Phoenix facility, most of these kids spent the majority of their lives in hospitals in their own communities and could in no way carry out or participate in a normal life program. In the cities where they grew up, they appeared sickly and looked emaciated, like prisoners of war or victims of concentration camps. They were fearful, touchy, allergic, and fussy eaters. Based on the descriptions of the physical state of these children in their home environment, it would seem that the atmosphere at the Asthma Research Center would be rather morbid and depressing, but it was quite the opposite.

The wondrous truth was that there was practically no indication that this was a place for sick children. The tone of the establishment was upbeat, and the children appeared exuberant and were generally healthy. Asthmatic symptoms and breathing problems were rare on the grounds, and the kids went to a normal public school. Many ate foods that they had previously been allergic to, and all participated in sports. For most of these kids, it was the first time in their lives that they had not felt different and inferior to other children.

Overall, the treatment program consisted of the following: The children lived in dormitories in groups with a housemother and were required to take care of their own property and keep their rooms clean and neat. There was a staff of medical experts who set up a specialized treatment program for each child, beginning with extensive tests and a diagnosis. Medical care was up to date and excellent. Along with this, each child was assigned to a psychologist who functioned as a personal counselor. It was the job of the mental-health personnel to establish a working diagnosis and to follow up the initial orientation period with regular weekly psychotherapy sessions. But the most essential aspect of the entire medical and psychological therapy was the children's separation from their home environment, where they were accustomed to being regarded as chronically sick. The interruption of the disturbed interaction and dysfunctional bond between the parents and their children was the key to the whole approach.

The unconventional "parentectomy," combined with the high level of medical care and psychological services, seemed to do the trick, but not for Lena. That's where our story begins. After a period of eighteen months, the doctors at the hospital were still unable to control her symptoms and had finally given up on being able to help her. In fact, she had become increasingly frail and was on the verge of death. The situation seemed totally hopeless. The consensus was that the best thing to do was to send her home to her family to spend what little time was left to her in a noninstitutional setting. The mood of her departure from the progressive research unit in Phoenix was one of utmost despair and futility. In spite of the rich resources available, they had failed on all counts and could not console themselves. All of the people at the hospital felt for the plight of this wretched little girl.

Coincidentally, I was leaving the hospital myself that same summer. I had just finished my work there and was about to start a private practice in Los Angeles. Lena was also heading for LA, and the staff at the hospital recommended that I continue her psychotherapy when she arrived home. I felt complimented by the referral but realized that I faced an awesome responsibility with little or no chance for a positive outcome. It would be a heart-wrenching encounter.

I went to see her therapist before I left, and she briefed me about this unfortunate girl whom I had never really known at the hospital. She described a somewhat-dwarfed, extremely bright and precocious child who was bitter and cynical. Medication and disease had combined to stunt her normal growth, physically as well as psychologically. Yet the therapist described a child of unique imagination and brilliance, who was a serious challenge because of her awareness and sensitivity. I was excited by the prospect of working with her, regardless of the depressing prognosis, but I was also plenty scared. I was just starting out in practice, and this case presented the most difficult circumstances—not just the immensity of the psychological problems involved, but also my own pain at the thought of facing her almost-certain death. The latter was especially unpleasant because it threatened to arouse my own death anxiety. Anyway, I was scared but game as I thought about our first meeting many miles away.

Lena was one of my first clients, and I planned to see her several times a week. Finally, the morning of her initial scheduled session came around, and it was time to begin. My heart was beating rapidly when I opened the waiting-room door. I saw a very anxious little girl who looked unhappy and who instantly captured my imagination. I was ready to love her, I suppose, and to fight for her. This was an instantaneous emotional reaction. I felt enormous compassion and would not accept the reality of her impending death. I knew that I would do everything to avert that outcome, and I felt that I was going to know her for a long time.

I had unusual faith in my approach, which was based in part on Direct Analysis, a developmental offshoot of more traditional psychoanalysis that confronted patients directly regarding their psychological productions. I had studied and worked with this approach back East while employed by its founder, Dr. John N. Rosen. We had applied the procedure in cases of advanced schizophrenic regression and had achieved promising results.

Despite my lack of experience and the fact that I had not as yet established a successful practice, I had a feeling of confidence about myself as a competent therapist. I maintained this assurance in spite of my youth and felt that my specialized training working with schizophrenia and my original theorizing as presented in my doctoral dissertation would help me to understand the basic dynamics of related syndromes. I thought that this would especially hold true in Lena's case because, the way I conceptualized it, both asthmatic and schizophrenic reactions derived from pain and frustration in the oral period, the earliest stage of psychosexual development.

My expectations in this regard proved to be accurate, and I was at home with this girl's thoughts and feelings and felt a special understanding. She picked this up immediately and, though we got off to a shaky start, we were able to establish a working relationship.

"Hello, Dr. Firestone, my mother and daddy told me that you—that you—uh, might—wanted to see me." She was wheezing heavily, and it was disconcerting because it sounded like each breath could have been her last.

"Yes, Lena, I did really want to meet you and get to know you. I heard a lot about you at the hospital."

"Yeah, but," her breath wheezing, "what's the good of it—I've talked to—so many doctors—the hospital," she continued slowly gasping for air, "Dr. Nathanson, with her teeth sticking out, saying 'What about your feelings, my dear? You must learn to confide in me.' Oh, there's no good to it." Lena sprayed her throat inhalator and breathed a little easier. I was put off by her painful asthmatic symptoms and mood of despair but maintained my interest and refused to become pessimistic.

"Look, maybe it will be different here. I feel that I can help you if you cooperate with me, and I want you to try hard," I said in a strong and persuasive tone.

Her stultifying response came immediately. "You'll follow me to the hospital and then to the grave." This statement of impending doom chilled me to the depth of my being. There was little hope or desire to live left in her. She really wanted to die and wished to be released from her torment. Her despair was clearly evidenced in her poetry. I learned in one of our early sessions that Lena had written several poems, and she reluctantly agreed to share them with me.

> These narrow walls reflect my whispered sobs,
> A witness to each pang of joy and pain,
> This quiet room my only sanctuary.
> Outside an endless battle sweeps the world,
> I lay here wondering if I am truly mad.

I felt her grief and cared deeply for this tortured child.

"Lena, let's get this straight. I feel that we can do something about this. If we really talk and trust each other, maybe we can understand why you have all this sadness and get these miserable asthma attacks. I think that your symptoms would be alleviated if we could get to your feelings. It's your bottled-up emotions that cause all the trouble. If you can't face the things you feel, then it comes out in your body instead."

"I sometimes see things, like I can't tell you. Right now I keep everything in uh—uh, a secret world ... "

"If you could let it out, could only let it out," I said.

"... a world where I imagine that my parents really adopted me, feeling like I was not like the other kids." She showed me another poem.

> I sit tethered to this bed,
> Watching as I am poked and prodded with needles,
> I wonder how some can look on in amazement
> And crave the kind looks and sweet words for the sick.
> Don't they realize the terrible cost of these small comforts?
> I pay with my body, my pain and my breath.

Weeks passed and she gradually began to open up. "I can't really talk about my parents. They are good people who really love me." She begins wheezing heavily.

"Then why do you feel that you are adopted? Something seems mighty fishy to me. You know what I think? I think you are the biggest sucker."

"What do you mean?" she asked, shocked by my remark.

"Like you're covering up for them, your parents, in some way. You don't want to tell the real story. Like you want to believe that they are good and all, and of course feel that you are the bad one. When you build them up, you tear yourself down."

"How? I don't really get what you mean."

"You deny your real feelings of anger toward them and they come out in your asthma. You attack yourself instead of them."

"You're crazy, Doctor, you really don't know what you're talking about. I sometimes don't like to talk to you." Her face looked mean. Even though I knew I was pushing her, I was a little hurt by her hostility.

Then, finally, her anger poured out and the wheezing stopped. Lena was angry at everything—her parents, me, her little sister, and everybody. At long last, the internalized anger and self-hate began to flow in another direction—outward. And it splattered all over the place. According to her mother, Lena became a real bitch at home. Lena told me her mother got so angry with her, she told Lena to answer her as "Yes, Mother dear," or choke. Very often, Lena obliged. I couldn't help being taken aback at her mother's choice of words in attempting to discipline her daughter.

In looking over my notes at the time treatment began, I described Lena as having a strong negative image of herself. This negative conception resulted primarily from Lena assimilating, or taking on as her own point of view, her mother's covertly rejecting attitude toward her. She told me that she had trouble turning off the nasty, self-depreciating thoughts she tormented herself with, especially at night when she was trying to fall asleep. It appeared to me that she ruminated a great deal, and so I encouraged her to try to be more explicit about her self-criticisms, to expose some of their content. She made an effort to say more, but it was hard for her, a real struggle. She was clinging desperately to this negative self-picture, and, at the same time, idealizing her parents.

Lena also found her hostile feelings toward her parents intolerable and was defensive and apologetic about them, preferring, on an unconscious level, to develop symptoms when these feelings were aroused. She would swallow her angry emotions, "choke on them," and internalize them to her own detriment.

Once during a session, she slipped up and criticized her mother, and immediately she became quite anxious and ill. She was especially reluctant to accept any inadequacies in her mother because her illness caused her, on a real level, to rely upon her mother for her very life. The utter dependency on her mother for shots, medications, and the like, complicated the young girl's situation immeasurably. Thus, if her mother were inadequate or "bad," Lena would surely die. Better to conclude that she herself was the bad one, because at least that offered hope for a possible change in the future. Perhaps if she atoned, changed her "bad ways," then she would be loved and safe.

Lena not only somaticized, that is, turned her negative emotions against her body, but she also was depressed because of her choice to inhibit her angry responses. That's why I called her a "sucker." I knew that if she could begin to accept her anger, like so many of the children at the hospital had learned to do, her physical symptoms would ease up. I hoped that Lena's depression would give way to a defiant and angry stage, allowing her to become freer from distressful symptoms.

Eventually, this did happen with Lena. Her anger came out and she began to feel better. However, this was not a smooth and continuous process. There were periods of regression and anxiety, followed by remorse and depression, and sometimes serious attacks requiring hospitalization and emergency treatment.

Once I was summoned to her side because she was failing rapidly. Her mother called and begged me to hurry over to their home. When I arrived, Lena was terribly weak and frightened. Alone with her at her bedside, I tried to get her to reaffirm her anger toward her mother, relating to a critical incident of the previous week, but it was to no avail. There was no response. Then, in desperation, I myself voiced the anger that I thought Lena felt toward her. I was scared of this approach at the time, but it just came out of me. I held her hand and tried to give her my strength as I mounted the assault on her mother's actions. Only minor improvement was noticeable. There was merely the slightest decline in the strength and rhythm of her wheezing. Finally, I had to go; and I left, discouraged by the lack of a positive response.

I went back to my office and returned to my regular duties. The phone rang, and it was Lena's mother. I was apprehensive, anticipating bad news and thought that probably the end had come. She asked me forcefully, "What on Earth did you do with her?" At first, I was even more frightened, expecting that she was angry, critical, or blaming of me, meaning that things must be pretty bad with Lena. Then I recognized that her voice was flushed with excitement, indicating gratitude, the polar opposite of what I had expected to hear. The news was good. Lena was feeling fine and her mother was thankful. She raved about my work and reported that I had accomplished a miracle. Another crisis had been averted.

The paradoxical situation was stupefying. What had I done with her daughter? I had helped her to face her hatred toward her mother so that she might live. The much-reviled mother was relieved of guilt and appreciative that her child had survived. I was existing in an upside-down world of unbelievable dimensions.

This event took place about ten months after Lena and I began sessions; and by then, we had developed a close relationship. One day, she appeared anxious and remote. She seemed to be heavily involved in fantasy and did not respond to our conversation. I repeatedly asked, "What's wrong with you, Lena? Why don't you tell me?"

Finally she answered, but fearfully, "You know how people think of things. I can't get this out—uh, you see, uh, you think—it's on my mind." She began to breathe hard, her chest heaving, and she spoke in a quivering, muffled voice.

"Try to say it," I encouraged, knowing that something important was transpiring.

"Well, you'll think I'm crazy or maybe really nuts, but I see this thing—and it really bothers me. But you won't like it."

"What is it that you see?"

"You won't believe this, but sometimes, well, I look up and there's, uh—uh, a thing, I mean a man's, uh, penis right in front of me. See, now you will really think I'm crazy."

I was relieved that she was able to say this to me. I had heard about this specific hallucination once before, but not with such a young child. I was familiar with its symbolic meaning on an oral level. I asked, "What do you feel like when you see it?"

"Sort of, uh, excited and mostly embarrassed and very scared, like I think I'm going out of my mind. Then after it, I feel dirty and bad, like a bad girl. Why do I think of such a thing? What's wrong with me?"

"When you see this penis in front of you, it's like an imagination that has become very real. It's not something wrong or bad, but let's try to understand what it is. What does it make you think of?" My tone was sympathetic, and I asked the question because I didn't want to make a premature interpretation.

"This is really terrible, you see, it makes me think of bad thoughts. One time I came into the bathroom and my—uh, you know, uh, father was standing there, you know, going to the bathroom—and I felt awful bad and . . . " Her voice trailed off.

"Like you weren't supposed to see him and were bad."

"Yeah—well, looking at a thing, I mean, a penis, is bad, like sex or something dirty. You know, in the jokes kids tell at school."

"What does a penis make you think of?"

"This must be nutty, but it makes me think of love or something, like food, but this is really weird."

"Say your thoughts."

"I was thinking of a lollipop—and some good things to eat," she said, and her face started to redden.

"It seems like a penis reminds you of something good to eat or suck on, of love and warmth. Who wouldn't wish to be well-fed and feel good and secure? When you see the penis, it's because of this wish to be loved and nurtured. Remember how you told me that sometimes your father is affectionate and kind to you when you're alone with him and your mother goes to her meetings? You long for his love, and that's part of the same wish that causes the penis hallucination."

She was obviously relieved to have gotten out these feelings and on subsequent days was happier and symptom-free. One day she said, "Now that I'm feeling better, I'll probably get run over by a truck." As is common, she couldn't accept the thought of real happiness. It was so removed from her established identity.

During the next couple of years, Lena went through many stages in her psychological development, and there were ups and downs in her asthmatic symptoms, but mostly there was relief. During one phase, she was enormously compulsive and ritualistic, planning her entire day and scheduling everything down to the smallest detail. These routines reduced her anxiety and acted as a punishment for sexual and aggressive feelings. Both kinds of feelings were accentuated and intensified by the oral deprivation she had experienced when she was very young. The exaggerated sexual preoccupation, as demonstrated by the repetitive penis hallucination, was driven by an emotional hunger for closeness.

Her emerging sexuality and strong sexual urges, responses characteristic of adolescence, were particularly frightening and guilt-provoking for Lena. It was an exceptionally difficult period for her. Sexual feelings originally directed toward the father are often focused on the therapist as a part of a transference reaction. Such was the case with Lena. She felt ambivalent toward me, very close, loving and sexual, then guilty and hostile. The compulsive rituals were her way of atoning.

Eventually, even the compulsive symptoms disappeared, and she was relatively free and well. However, it was a time of much emotionality as she approached puberty. This was a sensitive interval for her, and she very much identified with Anne in *The Diary of Anne Frank*. Lena felt a genuine kinship with this girl from a faraway place, who was going through basic changes in her femininity in an atmosphere of pain and persecution.

Lena was distressed about her looks, and she criticized herself endlessly for being short, "ugly," and "flat-chested like a stupid little boy." During one session where she happened to feel more open than usual, she found some relief from her more vicious self-attacks when she took a chance on revealing to me what she considered to be her most shameful thoughts.

Lena constantly compared herself negatively with her peers and was pointedly jealous of a close friend who was more matured.

The physiological changes in her body were hampered, and even distorted, by the medications she had consumed. Lena continued to be very small and underdeveloped for her age, and this caused considerable awkwardness when she was around boys she was attracted to. She felt that she couldn't compete with other girls for guys who interested her, and this caused her to feel bitter and resentful.

However, there was a problem of far-greater magnitude that compelled our attention. The medication that had saved Lena's life many times when she had severe asthma attacks in the past was a steroid derivative. This wonder drug had reduced her inflammation and preserved her life, but perversely it had caused many undesirable and insidious side effects. Let me note here in defense of her doctors that at the time that this drug was first prescribed, authorities were not fully aware of the dangers or ill effects of the miraculous medicine. Over an extended period, Lena had received massive dosages of cortisone in many last-ditch attempts to cope with her life-threatening symptoms. Repeated ingestion of large amounts of cortisone causes the adrenal cortex to atrophy, and eventually this can lead to death.

According to her allergist, Lena had to be weaned from steroids in order to have a chance to live. The danger was that if the drug were reduced too fast, she could suffer a bout of sufficient strength to kill her. In other words, due to insufficiencies of the healing substances in her own system related to the excessive use of cortisone, she could be completely overwhelmed by an attack.

We struggled with this problem for a long time, and gradually Lena was successfully withdrawn from the drug, and she became able to carry on a normal life. It seemed as though a miracle was happening, and everyone felt optimistic. But our joy was short-lived.

Suddenly, late one afternoon, I got a call from St. John's Hospital. Lena had taken ill, and her mother put her on the phone. Lena was screaming and yelling hysterically, "Help me, I want to live—I don't want to die!" She was in extreme agony and her anguished voice cut right through me.

I rushed to the hospital and burst into her room, but all was quiet. She lay there, silent and blue; she had lost the last great battle. I sit here now, with tears streaming down my face as I remember that moment. When I kneeled down to kiss her good-bye, I felt the full pain of life's perversity. When I had met Lena many years before, she was depressed and longed for death; and now she had died a horrendous death, screaming that she wanted to live.

I brought my precious little daughter, Lisa, to the funeral, and we watched from a distance as they lowered Lena's worn-out body into the open grave.

I will never forget her epic struggle.

CHAPTER 4

OFF TO A ROUGH START

TWO CASE HISTORIES

I was a young therapist just starting out in the first year of my professional life when I first met Victor Rombeck. He was a good-looking young fellow with a friendly demeanor, but I was shocked by his extreme nervousness and agitation. His speech patterns and expressive movements were accelerated to a level of frenzy that I had never witnessed before. He spoke so fast that I could barely make out the words as they flew out of his mouth. It sounded like double-talk or a tape playing at high speed, so that everything came out slightly soprano. I listened intently to try to establish communication, but my understanding was minimal. He was so racked with painful anxiety that I could hardly stand to stay in the same room with him. At times I could barely breathe or catch my breath. My heart would pound against my chest. I felt like at any moment I would join him in his disintegration.

In spite of my torment, there was something likable about Victor that made me want to stick it out. Month after month, I struggled to survive his meetings with me. Each visit left me trembling with a heightened pulse rate and severe tension in my back and shoulders. I wondered how he tolerated his stress without a further breakdown. Perhaps our sessions might help; after all, we were establishing a rapport.

There was one ironic element to his case. Victor had an incredible fear of heights, yet he worked as a window washer, which left him in cramped confinement high above the city streets. In his sped-up state of mind and body, it was a miracle that he never fell off the scaffold. It was torture for me to picture this bundle of nerves and churning emotions suspended at high elevations. I was amazed that it had never occurred to him that he might want to change jobs.

It was customary at the time for beginning therapists to undergo their own psychoanalysis. This was an exceptionally good idea, and I considered it an essential part of my training. I spoke to my analyst about Victor and complained about my anxiety and tension in working with him. Everything in me wanted to drop the case and recommend a referral because he made me so uneasy. My analyst cautioned me against that alternative. He felt that it was critical that I hang in there and come to understand why Victor was so disturbing to me. In his mind, it was too early for me to give up and quit.

Still, Victor's sessions were so uncomfortable for me that I longed to get away. As advised, I persisted and refused to turn my back on him. Staying present with him in the sessions calmed him. At first, progress was imperceptible; but gradually our interaction became normalized and we both felt less of the nerve-racking suffering. At long last there was therapeutic movement.

With Victor's anxiety partially allayed, we were able to dig into his underlying problems. They centered on his sexuality. He was embarrassed and tormented by the fact that he would have a premature ejaculation and therefore could not satisfy a woman. He felt extremely inadequate and was confused about his sexual identity. His jittery, overwrought state bordered on a full-out homosexual panic reaction.

It turned out that when he was young, his father had caught him masturbating. He forcefully picked up his son, pushed the boy down on the dining-room table and, holding a knife to his testicles, threatened to cut off his balls if he ever caught him masturbating again. Given his father's insane reaction, you can imagine the extent of Victor's castration anxiety.

Just before coming to me for therapy, he had met a girl he really liked; but he feared that he would lose her because of his sexual problems. He had been stalling about getting fully involved with her to stave off the humiliating outcome he feared. But he couldn't avoid the situation much longer without appearing strange and losing face. That's when he panicked. As he spoke, he looked sad and became tearful. The release of feeling further relaxed him.

As therapy proceeded, Victor confided more to me about his childhood and described his parents. "My mother was very mild and soft-spoken, but my father was a whole other story. What a bastard. He was always loud and mean and critical. He scared me. I think that he scared her, too. I never knew what was coming. We never knew when he would explode."

"How did that make you feel?"

"Just scared, like I told you."

"What about getting mad back?"

"Are you kidding? That would have been a disaster."

"I know what you mean, but you still couldn't have helped feeling hatred toward him."

"Yeah, I see what you mean, but it's hard for me to feel it, even now. Like I feel stuck."

I recognized from this and our other conversations that Victor's suppressed anger and rage contributed heavily to his intense anxiety reaction. I also realized that his father's brutality had affected his perspective about what it meant to be a man. He refused to identify with his cruel father and saw himself as a pathetic weakling by contrast. The confusion in his gender identification contributed to an ongoing fear that he might be homosexual.

In our sessions, I helped him work through his castration anxiety, and he gradually became more self-assured. He was terrified of his competitive feelings toward his father and had generalized that fear to other men. He learned that he had turned his aggressive feelings inward, thereby demeaning and attacking himself. The result was that he felt miserable, pathetic, and cowardly. Although women liked him, Victor never felt confident with them, especially in a sexual situation. He was never sure of his manhood. These issues comprised the core of our therapy focus for the next couple of years.

As he became more comfortable, his words became more understandable and he was able to express more of his feelings. I encouraged him to yell out his anger in the sessions, and he finally had the courage to get angry at his father. He felt tremendous relief and his overall mood improved. He started to feel what happiness was like.

At first, Victor's transference reaction to me was hostile and distrustful, but gradually he became more positive. How could he believe that I cared for him after his disastrous experience with his father? In time, my warm regard reached him and became a meaningful part of his life. After understanding and coming to terms with the source of his fear and working through the feelings of his transference relationship with me, he was ready to terminate our sessions.

Facing and releasing his anger was the transformative point in Victor's therapy. Victor's suppressed hatred toward his father, which he projected onto other people, led to ever-increasing states of anxiety. I became acutely aware of the value of clients identifying hostile feelings and expressing them in the therapy process. But more notably, I had learned an important lesson about life inside and outside of the consulting room.

Not only angry feelings, but all feeling reactions are significant, particularly the recognition and expression of one's sadness. When any feeling is repressed or held back, it fosters anxiety, and the resultant tension is only relieved when the emotion is released. The ultimate irony about sadness is that when people release it, they feel whole and unusually good; yet as children and later as adults, they attempt to avoid the feeling at all costs. Unfortunately, parents tend to suppress these emotions early on. The baby's primal scream must be toned down because it reminds parents of their own emotional pain. After a while, the child learns to conceal unhappiness to his/her own detriment.

Victor left therapy in a calm and happy state. He felt genuine affection for me and expressed a deep sense of gratitude. In parting, we both felt a poignant sadness. Later, he married his girlfriend and became an excellent source of referrals. That's when he introduced me to a friend of his named Tyrone Washington.

It's a strange phenomenon that so often beginning therapists are faced with some of their most complex and difficult cases. This was true of both Victor and the man he referred to me. Tyrone was a large man, about thirty-six years old, and he was built like a heavyweight prize fighter. When he first came for therapy, I couldn't exactly discern his motive for seeking psychological help. He was of a fierce disposition and lived his life on the edge of an explosive reaction. The client was a self-made man whose remarkable success in the construction business was based on an aggressive attempt to compensate for deep-seated feelings of inferiority. His parents were poor people, uneducated and unsophisticated. He described them as lacking in ambition, and he attacked them for "living like animals." In short, he was ashamed of them and passionately hated them for exposing him to a painful and humiliating childhood.

Tyrone acted tough and superior; he was suspicious, distrustful, and mean. It was hard to find anything likeable about him and virtually impossible to feel sympathy for him. Intellectually, I knew that he was a man who had been very hurt as a young person, but his character armor did not allow for a compassionate response. Instead, his angry eyes, seething manner, and hostile body language aroused fear in me, and my fear caused me to dislike him.

He had married his high-school sweetheart, an attractive, popular girl, when they were both eighteen. They had escaped their surroundings by running off and eloping. The couple had three children, two boys and a girl, who (at the time he came to see me) were nine, ten, and twelve years old, respectively. It was an unhappy family, completely dominated by this insensitive, tyrannical individual.

When we sat down in my office, he mentioned that Victor Rombeck had recommended me highly, and I asked him how they knew each other. He said that they had met in a class at night school and had started talking. They liked each other and had gone out for drinks a couple of times.

I asked him why he had come to see me, and he was noncommittal, saying only that he wasn't feeling that good. He told me about his poverty-stricken family life as a kid in a rough neighborhood. We talked some about his depressed feelings and made arrangements for two sessions a week.

In the second session, I suggested that he make himself comfortable on my couch and tell me his story. When he leaned back on the sofa, there was a prolonged silence, and I sensed that Tyrone was becoming increasingly agitated. Finally, he started talking, and to my dismay, he confessed that he was seriously considering murdering his wife. I wondered what in the hell I was getting into. I silently cursed Victor for his referral.

"I've been keeping up with the murder trial where that doctor, you know, you probably heard about it on the TV, had a scheme to get rid of his wife. Since then, I haven't been able to get it out of my mind. I guess I'm what you'd call obsessed. I know it's crazy. I'm constantly preoccupied with working out the details of how I could do the same thing."

"Why do you want to kill your wife? I mean, what about her is making you so angry at her?"

"It's a long story, but dammit, she nags me all the time—about money, about everything. I just want to shut her up."

While he lay on the analytic couch, talking about his hatred of his wife, his muscles flexed and he practically convulsed with rage. He looked particularly menacing at those times, like he might just lash out crazily and act out his violence on me. At other times during the session, he appeared quite cool and would meticulously try to work out nefarious schemes to do away with his spouse without getting caught. He was resistant to exploring his motives for wanting to kill her and preferred instead to discuss his plans with me. He took pleasure in imagining how he would outwit the law-enforcement officers, who he pictured would eventually try to solve the mystery of his wife's demise.

The sessions that followed primarily involved him talking about his fantasies of doing away with her. This seemed to fulfill a need in and of itself, almost like some sort of addiction. As you can well guess, this scenario caused me a great deal of grief.

According to the ethics of my profession, a psychotherapist has a duty to society and must warn any possible victim of his client's violent intent if he considers his client dangerous. However, if I notified his wife, I had the distinct feeling that she would probably do something that would be likely to increase Tyrone's rage toward her, possibly pushing him over the edge. I also sensed that if his intent were at an action level, he would not have been confiding in me. For the moment at least, he was just considering his options.

On the other hand, if I informed the police, my client would deny everything and their hands would be tied. There would be no real way that they could help. Furthermore, Tyrone would be furious at me and break off therapy, leaving no possibility of his getting help. My instincts told me that I could get him through this crisis without a violent outcome, but I knew I stood on shaky ground. If I had been wrong, I don't know how I would have dealt with my emotions. The decision would have haunted me for the rest of my life.

As in all situations, tragedy is mixed with comedy. In one session, Tyrone was talking about losing his erection when his wife farted while they were making love, and for some inexplicable reason, I responded with a wisecrack, "Gone with the wind, eh?" The joke actually amused him and, as he laughed, I sensed that the rapport between us was growing.

One day, Tyrone warned me that he might have to kill me

because I knew too much about his plans. I told him that I had discussed his case with all of my associates, so he would have to kill them, too. Even though I felt that he was starting to like me, I was still pretty wary of Tyrone's potential for violence. It kept me up some nights, the torturous thoughts of bloodshed and the fear that he had acted on his plan to kill his wife.

He told me that at times he enjoyed frightening and hurting people. He talked about holding his kids' heads underwater in their pool until they thought they were going to drown. Only when they writhed around in a last, desperate, struggle against suffocation and impending death did he release them. I couldn't listen to this sadistic story without registering strong disapproval, "Look, Tyrone, you're going to have to cut out this sadistic crap if you expect me to continue working with you."

He was angry and accused me of losing my therapeutic cool. He told me that he expected me to be objective and analytical and criticized me for my unprofessional outburst. I told him, "I don't give a shit what you think of me; I won't accept this type of behavior, and that goes for your destructive attitude toward your wife, too. I personally don't give a damn about any feelings of anger or hostility you talk about; any feeling is fine with me. But when you talk about acting out aggression, that's an entirely different story. Actions, even proposed actions, have consequences, and I won't tolerate any of it."

The incident passed, but I had made a major statement about limits, and he had implicitly agreed to play by my rules. That marked the beginning of genuine therapeutic change. I encouraged Tyrone to put his rage toward his wife into words and let out the associated feeling. He said that he hated that she was lazy and forgetful and absolutely refused to keep the house clean.

He yelled, "Let's face it—she's a slob, she doesn't give a shit about me." Then he added in a weak, victimized tone, "I tell her about it all the time, but she never listens. She should tend to her duties, you know?"

"Basically, you feel like she has no respect or regard for you and that brings up rage in you."

"Absolutely, like I'm nothing, you know. It hurts deep."

"I think that's the way you felt a lot of the time as a child. You told me before that your mother showed no regard for you and was cold and unapproachable."

"Yeah, it's the same crap all over again."

The strength of our relationship and his developing insight acted to support his weakened ego, thereby averting destructive action. The subsequent control he displayed permitted us to get at his underlying depression and work on his core issues. We were able to trace the roots of his hatred to the frustration he experienced as a young child with a cruel, emotionally frozen mother and a weak father who refused to defend him from her insults or protect him from her wrath. Needless to say, Tyrone's father had never offered his son a strong, stable male role model, and when Tyrone was eight years old, his father left the household for good. Despite his size, Tyrone was left feeling inadequate as a man, and he defended against his feeling of weakness by acting angry and macho. His mother was the only source of financial support, and he was entirely dependent on her for survival. Thus, he was fully vulnerable to her mean nature.

Unlike Victor, Tyrone gave vent to his rage, but as noted above, it was always combined with a victimized, even outright paranoid orientation. I attempted to cope with this pattern, but I knew I was entering into a potentially explosive exchange.

"You know, you always play the victim in your life. You always feel sorry for yourself. You're like a big baby."

"What the fuck do you mean?" I could feel him bristling, but I continued to probe.

"You act like a victim with your wife, always complaining about how she bugs you. You act like a victim with your kids, blaming them for being a big responsibility. You whine about your childhood, your parents and their being poor. In a crazy way, you're afraid to be cleanly angry. It's always mixed with the victim theme."

"You really piss me off, you know. What the hell are you talking about?"

"Look, anger is a simple, natural reaction to frustration. That's all there is to it. And the extent of a person's anger is proportional to the depth of the frustration. When you feel it simply as that, there's no problem and there is a sense of relief, but when you combine it with feeling victimized, you stew over it and there is no relief. It just builds up and you feel worse and worse.

"There are no 'shoulds' or 'supposed tos' about it. That's what gets you into trouble. When you can't feel your anger cleanly and it's contaminated with being wronged, you end up building a case about everything. Then you feel like a monster. You became so victimized by your wife's moods and her complaining that your anger kept building up inside you with no real outlet. Finally, you felt a need to kill her, and that was really crazy."

"Look, these shitty things really happened to me. You can't just forget it. My wife really acts like a bitch."

"Of course bad stuff happens, but it's the way you deal with it that makes it a thousand times worse. You're responsible for your own extra misery, not your wife or anyone else."

"I think I see what you're saying. The way I think makes it bad for me, not just what happens."

"Yeah, *you're* your own worst enemy, not the circumstances."

"You got something there, Doc."

Tyrone gradually integrated what he had learned from that critical session. He was much less tense and angry, and his life became more tolerable. What's more, he eventually eased up on his wife and kids. On one occasion, he surprised his family by offering to take them on an outing in the country. It was unusually relaxed and everybody had fun. Another time, he shocked them all by bringing them each a special present. He actually bought his wife a diamond ring.

There is one insidious twist to the story that reveals a profound and ironic truth about human nature. For many years, Tyrone's wife had stuck it out, accepting his abuses. When asked about why she put up with the mistreatment, she would cling to him in desperation, proclaiming a strong and everlasting love. Yet two years later, when Tyrone had developed in therapy, when he had markedly improved in how he treated his family and showed sensitivity and feeling toward her, she left him.

CHAPTER 5

DANCE OF DEATH

The rusty motorbike roared up Gladnell Avenue, past Amber Street, turned east on Langford Place, and screeched to a stop in front of a small white tract house. Brian Hoberman dismounted, scratched his buttocks, swaggered through the door, crossed the foyer, and headed straight for the kitchen. He grabbed some ham and cheese, slapped it between two pieces of stale bread, and his mouth was full when he first heard her enter the room.

Brian was eighteen. He had long, dark, stringy, hippie hair and his clothes were dirty and disheveled. His entire demeanor reflected a studied "I don't care" pose. In reality, he didn't feel much about his grimy existence. Passersby took him for a tough druggie, but he wore a kind of foolish-looking, friendly grin that was somewhat reassuring. The drug image was valid, though. He was heavily into marijuana and would consume bigger and better things when they were available. He was lazy, out of work, and short of funds. That's why he had come back to live with his mother in the shack behind the main house.

He could almost smell Sara's presence before he was aware of her footsteps. The hair on his arms was electric. He was finely tuned to her aura and could feel his body stiffen in response to her entrance.

The woman was crazed, staring off into space and actively hallucinating. Two months before, she had been released from San Antonio State Hospital, one of those cities of the damned, located in the suburbs of that city. During her stay at the institution, she had received a course of electric-shock therapy followed by heavy

doses of chlorpromazine, an antipsychotic medication. After set-
tling down some, she was sent home with a maintenance dose to
help her with any residual disturbing thoughts. Being of a defiant
nature, she refused to take her medicine, and this negligence pre-
disposed her to the auditory hallucinations she was experiencing
that morning.

At the hospital, she was diagnosed as a paranoid schizophrenic,
but unlike many of her fellow sufferers, there were meaningful seg-
ments of time when she was not only free of symptoms but actually manifested a humorous outlook. Her personality was such
that she was chosen as one of the demonstration cases presented
to students and visiting professionals. On these occasions, she provided entertainment to an otherwise cold and formal situation.

It was obvious that she had once been beautiful, with her
light-blond hair and lovely blue eyes. She had large, well-rounded
breasts and remnants of an exciting figure that had now gone
beyond full to fat. She was still seductive, and there was a puissant
sense of sexuality about her. At times, she was given to the histri-
onic, which added spice to the parade of psychological maladies
for her audience to ponder.

In the kitchen, there was a resounding crash as Sara accidentally knocked Brian's tin stormtrooper motorcycle helmet off the
sink, and it clanged along the tile floor. In spite of himself, he was
startled and accidentally spit some of the food out of his mouth.

She said, "Hello, Brian," taking him by the arm and making a
strange, cutsie face. "Don't you have a kiss for your mother?"

He hated her words, recoiled from her touch, and his body
spun away from her. His back was tense, shoulders up, and he felt
a slight nausea. He knew what her next question would be, and he
just wasn't up to hearing it.

"Did you get a job, honey?"

To pacify her, he mumbled some gibberish about opportuni-
ties as a salesman at Spencer Design Center. He hadn't even gone
out to look that day or even that week. Instead, he had spent his

time over at his friend Crazy Sam's place, getting high and playing his guitar. He had a new idea to play "Dixie" backward—thought it might be quite a hit. He had big ideas.

She was rattling on about the money situation and how he was of an age to support himself by now. He did his best to tune her out, but the sound of her speech in the background made his skin crawl like an animal being stroked in the wrong direction. He had to get out of there—he rushed for the bunkhouse in the backyard, crashed through the door, lit up a joint, and sank into a reverie on the overstuffed couch. He fantasized about getting his own place; he felt he couldn't last there much longer.

When Sara and his father had broken up, his sister, Anne, had elected to stay with her dad and was leading a good life. Brian couldn't picture himself in the disciplined, conventional patriarchal environment and absolutely refused to comply with the stipulation that he give up drugs. He couldn't bear the thought of living with the pain. He was too familiar with the aching, pulsating tension and sickly feeling. He was acutely aware of the menacing voices that beset him when he least expected. Besides, in some mysterious, misguided and perverse sense, he felt that he owed his mother some protection. After all, she always said that he was her little man. He had always stood by her, even when everyone else deserted.

Many years before, he had come by his parents' room and heard the sounds. There were moans and grunts and a lamenting, high-pitched cry coming from the other side of the door. In his innocence, he burst through the entry to investigate and found his mother in a flimsy nightgown, looking surprised and bewildered. She sat there, legs spread apart, perched on the edge of the bed, alone. When she recovered from the initial shock of his presence, she relaxed, appeared to shape a plan, and drifted back into a sexualized trance. He noticed that her face was unusually sweet and appealing. She was immersed in a pleasurable fantasy; her mouth was smiling, and she had never looked so exotic.

She seemed soft, and in a small voice, she coaxed him to sit on her lap. When the confused six-year-old boy obliged, he was surrounded by a warmth he had never experienced before. It was plush and comfortable, and he became aware of a new and interesting smell. The odor was compelling. Her voice was soothing as she took his hand and rested it between her torrid thighs. The aroma now reached a peak intensity that filled his world. Slowly she moved his hand back and forth on her soft, wet opening, and there was a surge of excitement in his penis. He felt giddy and high. Later, he noticed that his clothes were damp; he had broken into a cold sweat. When it was over, Sara stopped the swaying, sensual motion, leaned to one side, and then lay back on the bed. She cried softly and fell asleep.

Brian stole out of the room. The unfathomable event left him sexually bonded to his mother, and from that time on, he had a sense of being a fugitive. The solitary act had separated him from the rest of his family and his peers. He was no longer a part of the normal scene. He was possessed, no longer a free agent, and unquestionably, incontrovertibly he belonged to his mother.

Brian lay for hours, slumped on the couch in the back house, bathed in a dreamy state of euphoria. He woke up with a start. As his mind emerged from the haze, he was gripped by a powerful unease, a feeling of impending doom, a kind of unspecified paranoia. There was some sort of big, big trouble ahead, but what the hell was it?

Then his thoughts jelled and he remembered his panic that afternoon. It was intolerable to stay in the godforsaken house with his mother any longer; he would leave that night. But how could he tell her, and what would she say? How could he actually get away?

The slow, steady stream of consciousness ended when a booming voice buried deep in his soul blurted out the question, *"Why not kill her?"* For one moment, the simplicity of the solution fascinated and thrilled him. It made perfect sense; it had a kind of symmetry about it.

Seconds later, he was besieged by a savage terror that coursed through his entire being. "What kind of a sick thought was that? Am I cracking up, going mental like her? Am I fucking crazy, too?" He had to get hold of himself, get the stupid, demonic thought out of his mind. He must search out his mother, confront her about his leaving, and get the hell out of there. He stumbled from the couch, ran out the door, quickly crossed the backyard, and entered the kitchen, where he found Sara standing at the sink.

"Look, Ma, I've got to go this time. I don't feel that good here. I've got to try it on my own."

She didn't answer at first, seemed to be mulling it over in her mind. For one frightening moment, Sara knew how it would feel to be left totally and utterly alone. The thought was excruciating. She mustered up all her arguments, "You don't even have a job. Where will you ever get any money to support yourself? You never were any good; you don't have any skills!" Her desperation increased as he failed to respond to her appeals, "You can't make it out there. You think everybody is nice like your mother? You can't trust anyone; they'll shit all over you." Toward the end, there was a note of hysteria in her voice, and as a last resort, she grabbed him by the shoulders, her nails digging into his flesh. She held on with all of her strength.

"Let go of me, you fucking bitch!" he screamed, as he wrenched free of her grasp and ran for the door. At the front steps he caught his breath, weakened, looked back, and said, "Look, Ma, don't feel so bad. I'll call you next week." The fresh air felt good on his face as he rode away into the night.

The months rolled by. Brian got himself a room and a full-time job at a gas station. He was drawn to mechanical things, taking machinery apart and putting it back together again. He liked the sounds of powerful engines rumbling when he tuned the sleek, foreign cars. He fancied himself behind the wheel, rich and successful. His mind was gradually becoming obsessed with money, and he wanted his share of material things. He felt greedy and impatient and was starting to feel angry about his plight.

He spent his social time primarily with Crazy Sam and Sam's girl-friend, Linda. His friend's family was well-off, and when his mother and father were out of town, they had parties at his parents' pala-tial residence. Sam and Linda introduced Brian to Cindy Johnson, a pretty, new arrival in the neighborhood. They entered into a budding sexual relationship, but Brian was embarrassed, self-conscious and amateurish. She found him amusing and wild, but she laughed him off when he impulsively proposed marriage. Despite the romantic setback, the couple continued dating and things appeared to be going fairly well. Yet he still felt a certain emptiness, a hollow feeling in the pit of his stomach. He often thought about Sara, all alone in the Hudson Street house, and he felt a strange undercurrent of guilt, remorse, and missing all mixed together.

Sara had survived the outburst with her son and the sub-sequent breakup. She got a job working for her brother in his art-importing business. She attempted to sell the small array of artifacts that he had given her on consignment, by making the rounds of showrooms on San Pedro Boulevard and the small shops along River Walk, plying her trade. People took her for an eccen-tric, but a sense of pity and compassion led them to stretch in her direction and buy a few items. These proceeds, combined with a small amount of alimony, kept her alive.

In her free time, she tended to her real occupation—the intriguing enterprise of being schizophrenic. She engaged in a pathetic one-way dialogue with a popular rock star, whom I will call "Jon Henderson," while listening to his recordings from her extensive collection of tapes. She believed that Jon was singing directly to her. During the instrumental breaks, she imagined his singing voice morphing into spoken words meant for her only. At dinner parties, she played these imaginary conversations with her idol for anyone who would listen. The only trouble was that she was the only one who could actually hear the conversations between herself and Jon; everyone else merely heard the sounds of the accompanying guitar and drums when it came to the part where their verbal exchange supposedly took place. So deep was her preoccupation with her hero that at formal dinners, she actually set a place for the celebrity at the head of the table.

When Sara was free of her psychotic symptoms, her existence was wretched, hateful, and self-hating. She complained about her ex-husband, "the miserable bastard," and grieved over the loss of her children. Sometimes she wanted to give it all up and exchange the living death of schizophrenia for the real thing. She would cry fitfully on those black nights and, in her secret torment, would scream out for relief. Nevertheless, she was faint of heart and lacked the resolve and fortitude to put an end to her suffering.

Very often, on the days following those horrendous, nightmarish times, she would call Brian and complain that he never visited her anymore. Although she nagged unmercifully, it came to nothing. However, a strange set of circumstances, mostly events of the mind, brought the odd couple together again.

Brian's desire for money gradually grew into a mania about wealth and power. Grandiose fantasies in which he was a rich man surrounded by beautiful women became the order of the day. These imaginings increased in intensity when Cindy became interested in another guy and refused to go out with him anymore. Days at the garage became dull in contrast to his expansive daydreams, and his performance at work began to suffer. The boss became critical, then angry and threatening. The misguided young man began to feel that he was being persecuted; everything seemed so unfair. What had he done to deserve the wrath of his employer? To him, it seemed like a personal vendetta, because, from his vantage point, he was working as hard as ever. It was a negative spiral of compensatory fantasy, leading to deterioration in performance and low self-esteem, which of course led to bigger and better fantasies. He was increasingly dysfunctional and bitter. He thought about his parents and envied Anne for getting ahead in their father's manufacturing business. He nurtured a victimized feeling, which soon led him to demand his share of the spoils. He arrived at an amount, a percentage of his father's company that he felt he rightfully deserved, and he approached the old man. When his father flatly turned him down and told him that his demands were crazy, in effect telling him to go to hell, Brian stomped out of the office, filled with rage. He brooded about the situation and plotted his retribution.

He thought about Sara, and his mind began to focus on the house. Wasn't he also entitled to his share of the property as well as the stock in his father's company? Wasn't it only right and proper for parents to pass on their good fortune to their offspring? What about love? Aren't kids supposed to be loved? Damn it! He would do something about all of this! At least he could make his mother see his point of view.

About this time, Brian was at one of Crazy Sam's parties when an unusual incident occurred. One of Sam's friends was desperately in need of money and was beseeching everyone to buy his gun. It was a bright and shiny .38, and he passed it around the smoky room for people to inspect. When Brian handled the weapon, he immediately fell in love. He fondled it and felt a sense of power and destiny. Nothing had ever made him feel that good before; he had to have it. The demon inside him now had the means to achieve its objective.

Brian spent a good deal of his spare time at a firing range. He and his new buddy were getting acquainted. He loved the sharp retort of the beloved pistol when he pulled the trigger. The repetitive mini-explosions, the clatter of shots, and the wonderful noise were exhilarating, yet soothing. He felt a pleasurable sensation in his groin. The hours spent at the target range provided the release he was looking for. He and his new friend went everywhere together.

It was about time to confront Sara about the house. He wanted a signed document proving the legal ownership of his half. Something about the property gave him a sense of security like nothing else. Brian considered it to be his future home when his mother would die, and he wanted to nail down his rights.

The job at the gas station was a disaster, and he was on the brink of being dismissed. He had observed the boss talking to some new guys, and he concluded that he was about to be fired. The situation was growing more desperate. Things were happening fast in Brian's disordered mind, and he felt a sense of urgency. It was time for action. It must be done and it must be done immediately. He stroked the weapon in his coat pocket; it gave him the courage to face the upcoming confrontation with his mother and the confidence to assert his point of view.

The surprise visit from her son caught Sara off guard. At first, she thought he had come back to her because he missed her. When Brian laid his claim to the residence without a trace of affection or even a proper greeting, his request made her furious. He had no regard for her, she realized with a rush of angry feeling; he just wanted to exploit her, take advantage of her.

"Nothing here belongs to you, you ungrateful bastard. The only thing you ever come to me for is money. You don't give one damn about me. Well, for your information, I'm going to sell the fucking house!"

Sensing his underlying hunger, his quest for security, and knowing what the place meant to him, she savored her last remark. It was a moment of triumph and revenge for her hurt feelings.

Brian was struck dumb by her response. First, his mind reeled and he felt dizzy and faint. He almost lost his footing. "You tight asshole!" he screamed. Then the powerful rage welled up in him. He cursed her, reached for the gun in his coat pocket, and sprayed the house with bullets. He loaded, triggered the weapon, and reloaded. Pottery was shattered, broken glass was on the floor; there were holes in the walls, smashed furniture and debris were everywhere. Brian focused his attention and fired many extra shells into the recorder and the prized collection of the Jon Henderson cassette tapes.

In the violence of the moment, Sara found herself scared, yet excited, and drawn to the scene. Her head was clear, her mind quiet, and she felt oddly cleansed. Surprisingly, she registered the bizarre occasion as uplifting and strangely satisfying.

Neighbors, overhearing the gunshots, were shocked and frightened. It was they, not Sara, who alerted the police.

Brian fled the scene, only to be picked up later by the authorities and placed on probation for carrying and firing a gun without a permit. His mother, under pressure from her relatives, filed a complaint, and a court hearing was scheduled. In the vestibule of the courtroom while waiting for the case to be heard, the contestants went at each other with a verbal barrage. Conscientious friends of the protagonists separated them and insisted that Sara wait outside for her own protection. At the proceedings, a restraining order was mandated, prohibiting any contact between son and mother. While exiting the courthouse, the parties ignored the issue under dispute and came together in a frantic attempt to get in their last words.

Such was the powerful need for the couple to continue to conduct their ugly business that once again, the friends had to exert force to separate the two. When order was restored, Brian returned to his boarding-house room and Sara retreated to the safety of her family. Her brother and sister-in-law were cognizant of the ever-present danger to her life and suggested that she stay with them until things calmed down. She reluctantly submitted to their good judgment that under no conditions should she return to her home.

In the weeks after the shoot-out and court drama, Brian's mind was assailed by strange, surrealistic images. He had spectacular hallucinations and heard savage voices. His fantasies surpassed anything he had ever experienced while on drugs.

A vision of his naked mother flashed before him, as it had on that day long ago. Once again, he glimpsed her moist thighs and the swelling of her breasts. There was the familiar scent of her vagina and a lovely sensual feeling. He felt his penis get hard, throb, and ejaculate. The orgiastic pleasure was followed by a disgusted, vile self-loathing. His body contorted with shame and twisted on the bed.

"You are a mother-fucker, a real mother-fucker! A worthless scum. The lowest of the low!" He heard what sounded like his father's voice in the distance, calling out to him. The whisper turned into a shout. A cacophony of voices joined the chorus, *"You fiend! You fiend! You crazy, crazy man! You sick fuck! Only a psycho would think those kinds of dirty things. Who would shoot up a house like that? Don't you know what you are?"*

Brian tried desperately to defend himself, "I'm sorry, I'm sorry, I didn't mean it! I didn't mean it! I didn't mean it," he wailed into the empty night. Anguished cries poured out from his soul, "What can I do? What the hell am I supposed to do?"

"It's too late now," came the punitive voice. *"Way too late. You can't do anything right, never could. Everyone would be better off without you. Why don't you just kill yourself?"*

Brian had always been terrified of dying, and he recoiled from the awful suicide alternative with his entire being. There was a sharp reversal of affect. He was sick and tired of feeling afraid and self-recriminating. Suddenly, his thoughts became crystal clear and all tension drained from his body. The inexorable voice had spoken once again, reminding him of the perfect solution:

"Why not kill her?"

Only this time when he heard the familiar words, he completely took in the idea; it made perfect sense to him. He would get rid of the blasted visions once and for all and live in peace. Unconsciously, he stroked the precious gun lying near his pillow. The evil spirit was now totally in control, and the young man was cool and resolute.

Sara was bored living at her brother's house and had never gotten along with her brother's wife. She suspected that her ex-husband had had a brief sexual liaison with her sister-in-law, and so she had always been intensely competitive with the woman. As time passed, Sara's agitation increased significantly, and she yearned to return home. Curiously, her feelings had slowly changed toward Brian. She missed him and longed for a reconciliation. She even dreamt about him, and it was a happy dream. At supper one evening, she casually brought the matter up to her brother.

"Why can't I go back home? Things are quiet; the whole thing's blown over and I want to get back to work. Besides, I like being on my own. I can't stay here forever."

At this point, her brother exploded, "Are you crazy? What the hell's wrong with you? Can't you read the writing on the wall? He's going to kill you, you stupid idiot! First he shoots up the house; next it's you."

"Look, it's my goddamn life! I can do what I want!" she responded defiantly.

In his frustration, her brother pushed his chair away from the table and, giving vent to his despair, shouted, "What the hell else can I do? Go ahead, leave!" and that was that.

Sara was exceptionally cheerful on the departure day. She hummed a tune as she packed her last few items, and she maintained her good mood all the way up to her house. She chuckled as she looked at the overgrown yard with the massive rocks and her favorite prehistoric sculpture. She wondered if her pet snake had survived her absence.

Once Brian had made up his mind, he was determined to act on his plans straightaway. The voice kept pressing for action, *"Kill her, kill her now! Kill! Kill! Kill!"* It was a constant reminder. When he heard that Sara had returned to the house, he moved steadily toward the deadly rendezvous with his mother; there was no turning back.

Sara heard the bell ring, and she opened the door; he brushed past her into the living room.

"Brian!" she exclaimed cheerily. Then she looked up at his face. What she saw in his eyes was terrifying beyond anything she had ever known. She started to scream, but he had already called upon his friend. He shot her over and over at close range, pumping hot lead into her limp body. Blood was everywhere.

Drained of all energy, he collapsed on the floor beside her, his rage and hatred dissipated. The house echoed with an eerie quiet, the air oppressive and thick. Brian's heavy breathing and the faint ticking of the kitchen clock were the only sounds. He surveyed the gruesome scene in a state of confused disbelief. "Shit, what have I done?" His gaze settled on his mother's face, her expression in death transformed from abject terror to one of almost-peaceful repose.

A vague notion began to dance on the edges of his shattered consciousness. Then came the realization: He alone had been the instrument of her suicide.

POSTSCRIPT

"Dance of Death" is not based on voice-therapy sessions or on any other therapeutic interventions. Instead, it is an fictionalized account that illustrates the intimate connection between suicide and violence. Indeed, both tendencies often exist in one individual. In both instances the voice, which is an internalized critical thought process, plays a significant role in destructive actions. Internal voices act as a malignant counsel that derides and attacks both self and others. This inimical thought process is present to some degree in all people and to varying degrees has a detrimental impact on their lives. However, when these negative thoughts become the ascendant or dominant part of the personality, as was the case for Brian and Sara, they represent an active threat to the existence of the people involved. Psychotherapeutic treatment that takes into account the dangerous effects that these thoughts predispose is essential in order to avoid catastrophic consequences. One way or another, either through their own energy or that of concerned friends or family members, people in this type of crisis must receive help.

In voice-therapy sessions, we identify the underlying destructive thought process that is only partially conscious, uncover the source of the attacks, and support clients in planning constructive actions to counter their voices. These techniques have proven to be an effective approach to the treatment of a wide variety of psychiatric disorders. In addition, my associates and I have found that personality scales we developed, the Firestone Assessment of Self-Destructive Thoughts (FAST) and the Firestone Assessment of Violent Thoughts (FAVT), based on how individuals relate to a variety of negative thought statements, have been valuable diagnostic tools in predicting suicide and violence potential.

Last, when people become informed about the role that internal destructive thoughts play in their lives, they can better understand themselves and learn to control maladaptive behavior based on these voices. If these individuals run into trouble as they recognize and analyze their respective voices, they, too, should not hesitate to seek professional help.

In summation, voice therapy helps people differentiate from the self-limiting effect of destructive programming, and it contributes to their development into honest, independent, and compassionate adults. As I've written previously, "The therapeutic venture, by counteracting the dictates of the voice and disrupting fantasies of connection, offers people a unique opportunity to fulfill their human potential, thereby giving life its special meaning."[1]

We have only one life to live, why not make your life the best story possible?

CHAPTER 6

CONTROL

She was a remarkable beauty, a fact that instantly struck any man, or even woman, at first glance. Julia carried herself as though she knew it and liked it. She had long, blond hair and was strikingly curvaceous. Her breasts were accentuated by a push-up bra that emphasized her cleavage. She had a lovely face and a perfect figure, and she was every man's fantasy woman. She was the type that every woman envies and resents with immediate and open bitterness. It was as if God created this one without any flaws, including the way she moved.

I was late for my afternoon appointments because of a traffic jam on the freeway. I rushed into my office through the back door and, composing myself, headed for the waiting room. I was expecting a new client, a Mrs. Julia Coles.

You never know what you're going to see on the other side of that door, I thought. It's the first awareness you have of someone you will get to know in a most intimate and powerful way. And, of course, there will be a significant reciprocal impact.

When I opened my reception-room door, I was startled by Julia's beauty. I caught my breath and nodded to her, indicating that she should come along.

"Mrs. Coles, please come in. I'm Dr. Firestone."

I waited for her to enter. While accompanying her down the short hallway to my private office, I diagnosed her as a character disorder or borderline personality. This type of premature evaluation was a game I played to sharpen my perceptions. I first heard about this instant-diagnosis technique from an associate who had worked at the Langley Porter Psychiatric Unit in San Francisco, where the interns went through this procedure to hone their diagnostic skills. Actually, I wasn't too fond of diagnostic labels or pigeonholing clients and instead relied more on my feelings and intuition about the whole person. So I used the method just as an exercise to keep myself alert.

I could feel Mrs. Cole's tension and recognized that she was very high-strung. She carried a small, brown paper bag that I assumed had been recommended by a physician to help her if she began to hyperventilate. By covering her face and blowing carbon dioxide into the bag, then inhaling, she could gradually restore her breathing to normal.

"Please sit down and make yourself comfortable. I want to get to know you in order to be of help. First, tell me your full name, address, and marital status."

She began to relax with my easy manner and answered the routine questions. I gently probed into her symptoms and complaints in order to develop a historical perspective. I also tried out a few preliminary interpretations to establish rapport and see how she reacted. Her responses would tell me whether she seemed to be a good candidate for my therapy. I preferred to make this decision as soon as possible.

After the initial session, I decided to accept Julia as a client. I recommended a long-term in-depth therapy. I believed she needed extended treatment to cope with her narcissism and other character defenses. Three sessions a week were scheduled for an extended period. We discussed my fee and other practical arrangements. In parting, I encouraged Julia and offered some advice, "I really think we can make progress if we're absolutely honest with each other. It's reasonable to assume that your anxiety will subside when you come face-to-face with your real feelings. I hope you are feeling better from our talk, and I look forward to our next meeting."

"Thanks, Dr. Firestone. I do feel a little better. I'll see you on Monday."

We commenced the treatment program. In our first session, I described the process of free association to Julia: "Say every single thought that comes to mind. Don't censor anything, even if what you think seems foolish, illogical, or embarrassing. If you follow this suggestion as much as possible, we can discover what's causing you to feel miserable."

At first, Julia's conversation centered on her anxiety symptoms, and it was difficult to get at the root of her problems. After a few sessions, her hyperventilating was under control. When the full force of her symptoms abated, she began to delve more into her background.

"My mother is a dress designer and she's quite successful. She's pretty and says we're best friends, but that's baloney. When I was growing up, she couldn't find anything good to say about me. She complained about me being loud and told me that I'd always been a selfish child. She was so fucking mean and cold.

"My father is a whole different story. In a way, he was more nurturing and motherly. But was he stubborn! He drove like a maniac and scared the shit out of the whole family. We pleaded with him to slow down, but he never listened. He's a builder and project manager in hotel construction. Now they're divorced. When they broke up, he was a basket case. He cried and begged my mother not to leave. He threatened suicide. I was seven when they divorced. I was terrified."

"What did you feel at the time?"

"Like what do you mean?" She thought for a moment, then continued, "I felt, like, totally lost. But right afterwards, they sent me to boarding school and that was a lot better. I made some friends there and had some fun."

"You felt like things were better away."

"Yeah. Like I felt sort of okay there. I even hated school vacations when I had to go home."

In another session, Julia talked more about her current life, "People come up to me in the street and ask for my autograph.

Like, 'What do you do? Are you an actress or somebody? You must be famous!' Who am I? I'm nobody . . . I feel like nothing. I'm bothered by people."

"You feel like nobody. What's that like?"

"People don't even respect my privacy, gaping and gawking at me. Sure, I like it sometimes, but it gets to be a bore. The other day, I was in a restaurant with my husband—really, with my husband—and still a guy comes up to us and says, 'It's been such a pleasure looking at you, I would appreciate it if you would allow me to pay for your lunch.' Some idiots take my picture like I'm some kind of tourist attraction. Hell, yesterday I got stopped for speeding and the cop ended up asking me if there was anything he could do for *me*!"

She's right about attracting attention, I thought. The other day in the waiting room, two little boys, eight and nine years old, were pointing, whispering, and giggling about her. Another time, a client of mine came early to her session and saw Julia in the waiting room. She was stunned and joked, "If she's the client you see before me every week, I'm going to go home and shoot myself!"

"Everybody does everything for me, especially my husband, Ben. He thinks that I should make some sort of career out of my looks. It makes me feel like I'm retarded. I don't really feel that I'm good for anything or have any basic value. I'm plagued by all kinds of doubts."

"All of this attention must make you feel bad. There's a feeling that you don't really deserve it. I hope that you can come to give real value to yourself as a person."

Julia thought about that for a moment and looked sad. She closed her eyes and shook her head slightly.

"Yeah, that would feel a lot better," she said wistfully. "Think about my life. Guys are always saying that they love me, even my father's friend—and he's over sixty! How do you think that makes me feel? The other day, Martin, who works at my husband's office, calls me over and tells me he's got to talk with me. He confesses that he loves me and is so distracted that he can't work. He asks if there is any chance for him. These things make me feel so bad. I feel really guilty and sick to my stomach, really physically sick."

"It seems like you feel like a fraud or unreal."

"Yeah, I haven't done anything worthy of bringing out these reactions. My father always told me, 'You're a very special person because of the way that you're made physically. Everybody wants you; you're just a very pretty girl.' Is that all he thought I was good for?"

"My mother's attitude toward sex was so uptight. 'We just don't mention those parts of the body, dear. Be sure you don't show anything. Don't forget your underwear. How can you dress like that? Don't you have any shame?'

"When I was a cheerleader, we wore kind of sexy outfits and danced around. It drove my mother crazy. She would always say, 'I don't understand why somebody like you would get involved with things like that.'"

"Apparently your mother has negative attitudes toward sexuality. How did that affect you?"

"Well, it made me ashamed of my own sexuality, you know. I have a lot of guilt about sex. I have a lot of trouble with Ben, and I think he's disappointed with me."

"Disappointed? How do you mean?"

"I just don't feel relaxed during sex, and Ben wants to make love lots of times when I'm not in the mood. But if I decide that I want to be sexual, like if it's what I want to do that night, then I have an easier time relaxing. But those times are rare because I'm just not that interested, especially lately since I've felt so anxious."

During the session, I couldn't help looking at her. I mused to myself, *I haven't seen anyone, anywhere, who looked that good. What really incredible breasts—and no effort to hide them. I remember seeing sensational-looking women like her coming out of wealthy psychoanalysts' offices when I was a psychology student. Boy, was I impressed! Now this is my office and I'm in their place, and it really is a good feeling.*

My musings quickly returned to Julia. *Very interesting,* I thought. *She wants to be seen, yet she's ashamed. This is a clear example where the expressive features of the person do not indicate the underlying psychological stress or personal anguish.* Then I wondered, *Is she interesting because she's beautiful, or is she really interesting?*

In another session, Julia spoke about her fear. Once again, I encouraged her to speak freely. "I'm scared inside all the time, and I think that I'm really going crazy. I don't even know who I am. I can't seem to feel anything, only afraid. I can't stand this anymore."

"This constant fear has something to do with being afraid of your insides, of your inner feelings. It's your own feelings that frighten you."

"My feelings? Like what do you mean?" She paused. "It's really strange. I can't seem to feel the things other people do, but I used to a long time ago. Right now, I can't feel, and it's weird. If only I could cry or even feel sad. I just get very afraid and feel very cold, like I'm cut off from everyone.

"When I was little, I would get really mad, like when I was with my mother and I'd suddenly run in the street in front of cars. When I was older, I'd get in a car and drive a hundred miles an hour. I would feel good and free with the speed and all. It was, like, purifying."

"You know, from what you told me before, there is plenty for you to be angry about. But your angry feelings are terrifying to you. It's like you're sitting on a bomb. The fear of these feelings keeps you pushing them down, deep inside, and the pressure builds up. Then you have an attack of anxiety and feel like you're going crazy."

"You mean, like I've got to think about my anger more? Well, I do resent everybody doing everything for me," her voice rose and fell dramatically. "My husband's jealousy really bugs me, it really does. Ben has always been very possessive of me and jealous of everything and everyone. Now, since all of my physical problems, he keeps crowding me even more. Lately, I'm scared all the time, and I don't want to be alone. That probably encourages his overprotective responses, but I still hate them."

"It's no wonder you aren't able to breathe right; the whole thing sounds suffocating. It must really piss you off."

"You know, you're right. I feel like I never have any space. I really hate him and I hate my family."

In between sessions, I thought about Julia's problem. At first, her stylized speech bothered me. I thought, *She's always acting a role, all the time, games. This woman sounds phony, like those TV interviews of starlets, "Yes, the part in the movie is really me. It's fantastic!"*

She was able to control everyone around her—her parents, her husband, and all of the men whom she's seductive with. Julia manipulated people by utilizing negative power and weakness to get taken care of; basically, she controlled them all by maintaining a helpless, victimized, and childlike orientation. She was largely successful in this endeavor, but it left her feeling agitated and depressed.

Her every move is calculated and seductive, with those stray hairs curving around her adorable mouth, I thought. *Her blouse is always open just enough to reveal her breasts, an appealing picture. Say, you're not going to fall for her, too?* I wondered. *Hell no, I've got too much going for me.*

That's the answer I'd given my friend, Marty, when he asked, "How do you feel when you have a really attractive female client? Don't you feel sexual toward her?" I had replied, "Sure, but not to the point of feeling uneasy or nervous about it. I suppose a therapist who felt frustrated in his personal sexual life would be more uncomfortable."

Julia realized that I was impervious to her seductive ploys, and it infuriated her. She was used to guys falling under her spell. She had to be the princess, the one and only. Yet for Julia to have any chance of developing herself, I could not allow her to control the situation with me. She sensed that this was so and felt safe because of it, but she was also left feeling ambivalent. She was both pleased and annoyed.

"My mother taught me not to give anything to guys. She hovered over me when they came to the house. Really, every minute she'd come in and check up on me. They thought she was crazy. 'Get them to like you, but don't offer any sexual favors. That's the name of the game. Twist them around your little finger, but do what they want sexually only if you can't control them, and then, never all the way. Remember, never all the way. A nice girl only does that after marriage.'

"My life was like a circus with guys all over the place—coming and going. I'd lose track of even who I was supposed to be with. I'd give each of them a story and lie all the time. I couldn't remember who I told what. I just had to exert some stupid power over all of them. When I came to a party, I would size up the situation and kind of know that after a while, all of the men would be eating out of my hands.

"When my mother complained to my father about my crazy dating, he said that he hated all of the insanity. He said it would be better if I found a boyfriend and actually had sex than to continue with this menagerie. His remark really pissed her off; my having sex was her worst fear.

"I always dumped my troubles with my boyfriends on my parents. My father said that he lost all faith in me and affection for me when I was around sixteen. That's when I started that wild dating."

While describing Julia's chaotic romantic life in a case conference, I made a funny association. I remembered a similar spectacle from my college days, "All of the male dogs in the neighborhood were camped around my house in Berkeley when my dog, Frisky, was in heat. They would pace back and forth, sniff each other, fight, and in desperation even mount each other. It was a tragicomedy, an ongoing melodrama of sexual frustration. There were often ten or fifteen dogs about the place. When we would open the door, they would all come to attention and focus on the lucky people who were close to the object of their sexual lust. To exit safely and get free to go to school, we had to throw rocks to scatter the crowd. While passing among them, I would address them with, 'Good morning, gentlemen.' I tried to lose them on the way to class by going into one door of a building and out another.

"One medium-sized red dog with a square face was the most persistent of her suitors. We called him 'Asshole,' or 'AH' in the event that there were people around who would be offended. He was totally brave and fearless. If we were driving with Frisky, he would actually jump through the window of our car while it was moving to get near his love. If he was walking with us, he would be protective, immediately attacking any male dog that came near her or us."

I enjoyed telling the story. It provided an amusing break in the sad and pathetic narrative about Julia's life.

In one session, Julia said, "Karl was the only one I really cared for. We didn't really go all the way sexually, but, well, we did everything else. He was the one that, do I have to be specific? Well, we played with each other and lay around without our clothes and were really excited. We were tremendously turned on by each other.

"You're not gonna believe this, but I'm pretty sure his father was high up in the Mafia. Karl kind of intimated it when he talked to me. Boy, was he crazy and wild! We drove really fantastic cars and went fast, really fast. But it was actually too wild. We could have gotten ourselves killed. He even hit me a couple of times. He did a lot of drugs, and once I had to take him to a hospital. I remember the doctor coming out of the exam room, dropping all of his papers nervously, and muttering, 'This kid is really too much.' But, look, I really loved him, I mean with honest feeling. Like he still calls up once in a while to find out how things are with me. He always asks if there is any chance. I still dig him, but it's too crazy, the whole thing was too crazy. He finally cracked altogether, and they had to put him in a private hospital for mental cases.

"During this whole wild time period, my parents sent me to a therapist in town; he was actually pretty groovy. I liked him, but my mother got rid of him and said that she could help me better. What happened was, the man told my mother that it was better to give me my freedom to go out with Karl, even if I got killed, than to confine me and stifle me. My mother felt that the therapist was cold and insensitive and had no real feelings if he could say something like that. Of course, now I see that the man was just making a point and that he was right.

"Anyway, with all of this commotion, the wild crazy life with Karl and the thousands of guys all over the house—it was driving my parents crazy, I mean really crazy. That's why they kind of pushed me toward Ben. He also had money and was the son of a successful businessman. He was the opposite of Karl. He was exactly what my parents wanted, someone who was safe, a 'good' man. He acted just like a mother toward me: kindly, protective, and he was easy to manipulate. Damn, they really pushed this marriage on me. I remember my honeymoon in Mexico was a complete disaster sexually and otherwise. Ben was always jealous. He had good reason. I kept thinking about Karl all the time, thinking to myself over and over, 'I'm sorry, Karl, I'm really sorry.' I felt like crying all of the time."

At times in therapy, Julia would be mean or explosive either toward me or herself. She could be quite savage and spiteful: "You'll regret the day you ever took me on as a patient." "I really can't stand you, Dr. Firestone!" "I feel sorry for you, you're such a nerd." Or, "I'm just no good. I'm never going to get better."

Toward the end of one session, Julia was acting more seductive than usual. She told me that she really liked me. She said that she wanted to stay on for an extra hour because she felt she could "really be productive." I told her that, personally, I wouldn't mind continuing the session. I said that I liked being with her, but I didn't feel that it would be a good idea for her therapy. She quickly retorted, "Well! If that's the way you feel, fuck you!" and stomped out of the room.

Later that evening while sitting with my wife, I had an uneasy feeling. I apologized to her for being so self-absorbed. "Don't worry about it," she responded. "Do you want to tell me what's happening?" I confided that I felt that one of my clients was in danger and I was concerned.

Just then, the phone rang and it was Ben. His voice was trembling as he told me that Julia had locked herself in the bathroom with a knife. She was threatening to harm herself if I did not give her an extra appointment the next day. I told him to try to get her to open the bathroom door and put her on the phone. Ben put the receiver down, and I could hear a commotion in the background. When Julia finally took the telephone, she railed at me and begged me to see her the next day, or she would kill herself. Under ordinary circumstances, I would have been glad to accommodate her request. It was of little or no consequence for me to arrange an extra appointment, but I knew that if I let her control the situation, it would completely eliminate any possibility of a positive therapeutic outcome. I weighed the situation in a careful and sober manner. In the end, I was unwilling to concede to her demand, which was stated in the form of an ultimatum, and I refused to see her until her next regularly scheduled appointment. I told Julia that I really cared about her and did not want her to hurt herself in any way, but she would have to wait. When I hung up the phone, I was thoroughly shaken.

The phone rang a minute later, and it was Ben again. He was distraught that I had not obliged Julia, and he was afraid that she would act on her threat to kill herself. I was worried, too, but I trusted my clinical judgment that she would not do it. I tried to explain to Ben about the tyranny of the sick, "You can't let her rule you by her threats. Acting on your fears and indulging her would accomplish nothing in the long run, because if someone actually wants to commit suicide, no one can stop them. In fact, by catering to them, you make this type of vindictive behavior more likely, not less."

Ben could not comprehend this argument. He thought that I was professionally irresponsible, calloused, and unfeeling. I had second thoughts that I should have had Julia hospitalized both for her own protection and for my own peace of mind. I realized that I faced one hell of a mess if I was wrong. But luckily, the entire incident passed without further complications, a fact that boded well for Julia's future well-being.

Nevertheless, the dramatic episode led me to conclude that it would be advisable to see Ben in sessions in order to help him support and strengthen her impulse control in the home environment. If he could manage to stand up to Julia and not accept her abuse, it might serve to limit her acting-out behavior and reduce her tendency toward guilt reactions and self-recriminations. This would facilitate my being able to uncover the deep-seated repression that fed her underlying depression. My meetings with Ben were effective and turned out to be a valuable contribution to Julia's therapy.

While laying out the case to my associates, I interjected some personal material about my own reactions: "I used to be more of a victim of other people's suffering and their manipulative forms of blackmail. One experience that really helped me with this was when I had a bicycle accident where I all but tore off my little finger. When I was in the hospital after the surgery, I was drugged to relieve the pain. When I got home, the morphine gradually wore off. The doctor had given me painkillers to take at home, but the pills made me feel nauseated and weren't powerful enough. The pain built up to where it felt like somebody was bending my finger back full force. It went on and on for hours. Like my clients, I felt an almost-insane feeling of rage toward my doctor for letting me suffer. I wanted him to take care of my pain, even bear it himself, or at least care desperately about it.

"It was at that point that I realized the sheer stupidity, injustice, and futility of wanting someone else to take over your suffering. It serves no purpose other than to disturb and provoke others, who have their own hardships to bear.

"I began to understand that I was accepting too much responsibility for the pain of my clients. This not only affected me adversely in my own struggle but was essentially disrespectful to them. In a basic human way, it was intrusive; it invaded their boundaries and in some way infringed on their experience. Maybe it doesn't seem connected, but insights like this, together with a greater respect for my own worth, have helped me to cope better with suicidal crises in my clients. In this example, even though Julia's behavior was more melodramatic than self-destructive, it was still potentially dangerous; there was always the possibility of her accidently harming herself. It was crucial for both of us that I had matured in this facet of my personality and did not submit."

During our next session, I explained to Julia, "You see, every time you get angry, you don't stand up and fight like other people. Instead, you back off and try to get revenge by doing something wild and self-destructive, like running in the street, driving a car dangerously, or just feeling terrible and depressed. As if you were saying to your parents, 'Look what you've done to me,' or 'You'll be sorry if something really happens to me.' Sure, they get bugged by all of these things and it upsets them, but it's just not worth it. It's never worth getting even with other people by hurting yourself. There are much better ways of getting angry.

"The other day, when you asked me to stay an extra hour and I refused, you found you couldn't get me to do everything you wanted me to do. That night you locked yourself in the bathroom with the knife in an attempt to punish me; you wanted to get even with me for frustrating you by not complying or knuckling under. What a dumb way to try to get at me. Sure, I would have felt bad if you had hurt yourself, but what about you? You would have been totally obliterated. I would have felt compassion for you, or even angry at you, but you would have been dead. That's pretty crazy, isn't it? Remember, it's never worth it to manipulate others at your own expense."

"I'm beginning to see what you mean."

"There's more to it. When we are young and when we're hurt, we need to depend heavily on taking control. Later, control is our enemy; it interferes with living a free and honest life. Things work out for us so much better when we are vulnerable and not defended or controlling. It gives people a chance to love us, because in that state, we are actually more lovable."

"I guess I just need to learn to be myself and stop worrying about what other people think. I know that I am always kind of on guard."

My words appeared to reach Julia, and she became more open and trusting in the sessions that followed. She manifested less of a defensive attitude and was more expressive of her feelings. It culminated in her sharing an interesting and valuable release of personal and sexual material, along with key insights into her life.

"The other night," Julia recalled, "I was angry at Ben and I went downstairs to get a sandwich. Suddenly, I was shocked out of my mind. I had a vision of this Japanese samurai, all muscular and standing like in a karate stance. He looked evil, and there was blood all over his face and hands. Then I noticed it. He was holding a knife and was going to kill me. I was terrified and couldn't stop screaming, 'Please don't cut me up!' Ben heard my screams and ran downstairs. I saw blood all over, like I had a vision of my whole downstairs all blood-soaked. Blood on all the furniture and all over the rugs."

"What was cut? How were you hurt?"

"It's really weird. I've always been fascinated by knives, but terrified of them, too. When I was a kid, I was afraid of being attacked by a man with a knife. I guess Mother always reminded me of that danger. I just had a funny thought. Like I have a cut, sexual like, but this is crazy. Somehow, it makes me want to laugh. Hey, like blood, like the menstrual flow, like a wound. Hey, maybe that's why the Sharon Tate murder was so scary to me, like I'm going to get punished. I'm going to be killed by some weird, insane spirit because I have a vagina. Like both of them, my mother and my dad, will murder me if I'm a sexual person."

"Why would they want to hurt you for being sexual?"

"Hell, I don't know ... for different reasons. You know, I think that my mother was always jealous of me and wanted to get rid of me. For all the fuss she made over me and her bullshit talk of a special love between us, I never really trusted her. I think she wanted the attention for herself. I think that's why she was always telling me those weird things and warning me against 'going all the way' with the guys I was dating.

"Maybe that's why I can't relax during sex—I still hear her warnings in my head, and then I tense up. But like I said before, if I'm the one who decides we're going to make love, then for some reason, it's better. Maybe because I'm calling the shots and everything is under my control, like the timing, and, you know, even the way we do it, the positions. But somehow it doesn't feel very good. Afterwards, I feel even more guilt than other times. It's kind of like what you said, control is my enemy.

"On the other hand, my dad was very possessive of me, like I was his little girl. He never did anything to me, you know, sexually, but he always looked at me funny. I felt safer with him, but I wouldn't be surprised if he had ideas." Julia paused for a few moments. "Starting to figure this whole thing out feels like a relief to me. It explains a bunch of stuff."

"You seem to have uncovered the source of your fear of injury. It ties in with your fear of retaliation for being pretty and winning over a sexual rival or for being a sexual woman. I think you're getting somewhere."

"Yeah, I'm beginning to see how everything kind of connects."

She paused again and this time looked directly at me. I sensed that she was really seeing me and not just looking to get a reaction . . . not seductive at all, she looked vulnerable and open.

"You know, I feel pretty close to you, Dr. Firestone. I really look forward to our talks. I know I'm not as important in your life as you are in mine, and I guess it makes me mad. But it's great to be able to feel and to let somebody matter to me. Some feelings are painful, though. Maybe that's why I shut them off."

I felt warmly toward her and was glad to see the progress that she was making. "I'm glad that you are becoming more aware of your feelings, and I care a great deal about you, too. If you can learn to tolerate your loving feelings and feel them here, I'm sure you will be able to love someone in your life. Maybe those feelings will carry over to Ben or, if it doesn't work out with him, with someone else."

"Yeah, like starting out again, only maybe this time, I'll have a better chance at it. I'll see you next week, Dr. Firestone."

AUTHOR'S NOTE

In telling this story, I used the word *control* to refer to Julia's manipulations of other people, which I did not allow her to act out with me. In *The Ethics of Interpersonal Relationships*, I addressed this issue: "Some people consciously or unconsciously use self-destructive behaviors to gain leverage over an intimate partner. Threats of self-harm, bizarre risk-taking behavior, or actual suicide attempts are especially frightening. These maneuvers effectively imprison both parties. The more insecure the partner is, the more the need to control and manipulate the other."[1]

CHAPTER 7

THERAPIST OR TYRANT?

I was eighteen, and it was the summer break after my second year as an undergraduate student at Syracuse University. When I returned home to Brooklyn, I badly needed to find a job. I had the idea of working at a mental hospital as an attendant, which had a double advantage: It would enable me to pursue my newfound interest in psychology, and it would also impress my old gang. To my friends, it appeared to be a courageous enterprise, because they were spooked by the idea of a "lunatic asylum." I sensed that they would look up to me for the challenge I had taken on. Actually, I was more than a little scared myself.

It was not an easy job to find, but eventually I was hired to work on the disturbed ward in the King's County Hospital's Psychiatric Division. Patients were admitted directly from the city streets. Many were incarcerated during the evening and, almost immediately upon admittance, were placed into straitjackets. They generally spent an abysmal night in a cramped cell in the summer heat and woke up the next morning in frightening and unfamiliar surroundings. My task was to release them from their straitjackets, shave them, and see to it that they were showered in preparation for their medical examination. Needless to say, many patients woke up angry, even belligerent. To make the situation worse, the shower room was slippery and dangerous, as the tiled walls and floors were very hard. I quickly learned to free one arm at a time from the restraining apparatus so that if the released limb attacked me, I could replace the ties and be safe from further assault. This precaution was no laughing matter. During my apprenticeship at the hospital, an attendant had been strangled to death by a patient who had escaped from his straitjacket and used it to kill.

One afternoon, a huge brute of a man was admitted and placed in an isolation room. I peered through the door's observation panel to get a look at him in the hopes that he wasn't a dangerous psychotic. At that moment, the man awakened from his sleep, rose up to his full height, turned toward the bed, and urinated. Once finished, he let out a deep sigh, plunked himself back down on the wet mattress, and fell asleep. I was relieved to diagnose him as an alcoholic sleeping off a bender.

There was a big problem in the hospital regarding the reliability of the attendants. The job paid poorly and did not always attract the best element. Many of the men who had been hired were not motivated, and their attendance was sporadic. I worked in the section of the psychiatric hospital reserved for the most severely disturbed patients, where there were periodic outbursts of violence. Control was easily established when all of the personnel showed up, but it was dangerous for everyone concerned when there was an insufficient number of attendants on the premises. Three or four men could cope with the aggressive behavior of a violent person, whereas with only one or two attendants present, there was always the risk of the attendants being hurt themselves or accidentally injuring the patient. I would arrive at the hospital early and pray that enough attendants would come to work to make for a relatively safe and comfortable day.

My memories of the time I spent at the hospital are full of disturbing images. I remember the pale lime green walls, my feeling of apprehension, and my awareness of real danger . . . a violent battle with a young female patient who had attacked the nurses, her naked body totally immersed in sweat, constantly slithering and sliding out from my hold on her . . . carrying a recalcitrant Mr. Jean Paul, kicking and biting, down the hall to receive his medication . . . a wild man who had suffered severe burns riding his motorcycle through fire in a crazy, manic state . . . the snake boy who undulated rhythmically and whom I fed on the upswing of the cycle . . . a man who would run into a stone wall headfirst but who agreed to remain quiet if I promised to beat him up later . . . Ted, a large, deranged individual, who would sit on the window ledge and masturbate during visiting hours, spewing his semen at the unsuspecting relatives . . . an idiot savant with huge testicles and a small member floating on the mass of flesh, whom I had to bathe daily . . . the fights I had with tough, insensitive attendants who were sometimes sadistic in their treatment of the patients . . . my envy of the doctors and their important role on the scene . . . my nightmares after days spent in these chaotic surroundings. I often chuckle when I think about how, in spite of the harrowing circumstances, my teenage appetite was so ravenous that I ate off the opposite sides of the plates as I fed the bedridden patients. In addition to the painful impressions of the hospital environment, I also have poignant memories and affection for the unfortunate individuals who were in my care.

Although I had always been interested in psychology and fascinated by people, prior to this time I had had no psychiatric training. I was not prepared in any way and had no understanding of mental aberration when I started working there. Toward the end of this strange summer, I had become adjusted, even accustomed, to the hospital environment and was asked to train new attendants for the job. I had an uncommon feeling for the patients and attempted to communicate my point of view to the newcomers. As the summer came to an end, I felt sad to leave this setting. I felt a strong affinity with and empathy for the suffering humanity, and outrage at the tragic circumstances that had produced persons so hurt and distanced from themselves.

Now it was five years later. I was a graduate student working with Brodsky when I coincidentally received a letter from an old friend and fellow student, Pete Weinman. He wrote that he had become familiar with the work of a psychiatrist named Dr. John N. Rosen and had applied for a job at his treatment center in New

Hope, Pennsylvania. He had been accepted for the position and would begin to work there in the spring.

Dr. Rosen's book, *Direct Analysis*, delineated an interesting theory and innovative psychological-treatment approach to schizophrenia.[1] Pete was impressed with Rosen's courage in utilizing psychoanalytically based therapy techniques with schizophrenic patients, because Rosen's work contradicted a firmly entrenched attitude in the field that schizophrenia was a medical problem and impossible to treat psychologically. To the contrary, the psychotic individuals under his care responded well to the new and promising methodology he had developed.

I wrote back to Pete about my therapy with Brodsky because it seemed comparable to Rosen's work with psychotics in a residential milieu. Pete responded and asked my personal opinion about Rosen's contribution. The last two lines of his letter (paraphrased here) genuinely touched me: *I admire your understanding of psychology and consider you a trusted friend. I hope that someday you will join me at Dr. Rosen's facility and we can work together.*

After reading the material, I concurred with Pete's view that Rosen's work was admirable. I respected the psychiatrist's forceful personality and remarkable compassion in working with cases of catatonic excitement. These seriously disturbed patients were completely immobilized, but they would suddenly break out with an action, which was often aggressive. They were driven by intense fear, exhibited high fevers that led to total exhaustion, and were perilously close to death. Nothing could stop their inevitable decline. Rosen had spent countless hours at the state hospital in close contact with these seemingly hopeless patients. Although they were considered to be terminal and beyond any form of human communication, Rosen met them face-to-face and, in effect, entered into their psychosis with them and led them out. With his ingenious therapy technique, he had saved their lives and had eventually gotten them through their crises. I had never before read case histories that were more dramatic. None involved such absolute self-sacrifice on the part of the therapist in terms of time spent, personal involvement, capacity for intuition, and sustained professional application.

Rosen liked Pete, and he had become a psychotherapist in Rosen's residential treatment program. As soon as there was an opening for a similar job, Pete suggested that I apply. He told me that if I wanted the job, he would be glad to put in a good word for me. I immediately responded affirmatively, and I acknowledged my gratitude to my good friend. I knew that if I were accepted, I would have the opportunity to observe and treat seriously disturbed patients at close quarters, and it would offer me a unique chance to implement my therapeutic skills and develop a comprehensive understanding of the psychoses. Furthermore, there was the opportunity to study with a forward-thinking figure in the field. Within two weeks, Pete notified me that I had been accepted for the position and that I should report to the Bucks County facility in June. Needless to say, I was delighted and it was a cause for celebration.

Summer rolled around, and it was time to leave Denver for my apprenticeship with Dr. Rosen. I had passed the comprehensive exams and hoped that my work back East would fulfill the necessary requirements for my internship, one of the last steps toward acquiring my PhD.

Having finalized the arrangements, packed up books and clothes, and worked out the travel itinerary for both Louise and myself, I boarded the eastbound Union Pacific; sadly, I would have to travel without my wife's companionship, because she had to conclude her duties at school. She planned to drive our car out to Pennsylvania two weeks later.

The big diesel engine fired up and the long streamliner pulled slowly out of the station and gradually gained momentum. I found myself sitting by a window with my forehead pressed against the glass, looking out as the landscape rushed by. I was off to another adventure, one that would surely have a momentous impact on my professional life.

The plan was to meet up with Dr. Rosen in New York City and then travel with him to his compound in New Hope. After arriving at Penn Station, I headed for King's County Hospital in Brooklyn, where Rosen was giving a presentation. It seemed like fate that I would meet him at the same institution where I had worked some years before as a lowly attendant. At twenty-three, I felt proud to be returning as a professional.

Rosen was talking to a large group of psychiatrists in the main lecture hall when I arrived, and I was met at the door by one of his assistants. "I'm sorry I'm late, but my train just got in and I came straight over," I said apologetically. The assistant, Peter, shrugged it off and said that it was no big thing. Peter was a tall, handsome, blond-haired man who was Rosen's personal assistant. He was pleasant as he ushered me to a seat in the front row of the auditorium.

When I sat down, Rosen was up on the stage. It was my first glimpse of the great doctor. He had a rugged look about him and was of medium build. His words blasted loudly throughout the lecture hall. Toward the end of his speech, he was talking about the work done by recovered schizophrenics who were now serving on his staff. In a dramatic gesture, he pointed me out and asked me to stand up. Somewhat confused, I was obliged to be cooperative, so I stood up. Dr. Rosen addressed the audience, "Now, would anyone in this assembly consider this man to have been schizophrenic?" I was astounded and mortified by the implication was that I was one of his recovered patients who was now working on his staff. As I sat down, I felt a rush of hatred toward Rosen for using me as a ploy in his deception. I immediately lost a great deal of respect for the man and thought of him as a phony and a showman. I was so disillusioned, I was temporarily speechless.

When the lecture was over, I was swept up into Rosen's entourage and was astonished by the audience of well-respected psychiatrists fawning not only over Rosen but over me as well. One of the doctors even offered to carry my coat as we exited the auditorium. I thought to myself that this was a very fucked-up world.

Peter pulled up to the hospital entrance in a shiny black Cadillac. I started to get into the front seat but was informed that it was Dr. Rosen's seat and that I should ride in the back. The drive along the Delaware River, the beautiful manicured farms, the lush green pastures, and the quaint town of New Hope were pleasing to the eye. As we drove along, Rosen said, "I really showed those idiots something today, didn't I?" The remark was as much for my benefit as for Peter's. "They don't know a damned thing about schizophrenia, with their traditional views. Those blind jerks are in the Dark Ages." Rosen did not seem at all like an accomplished psychiatrist; he struck me more as a General Patton type.

During the ride, he asked some basic questions about my background but showed only a perfunctory interest in the answers. As for me, I felt uneasy about the situation that I had gotten myself into. I was even a little angry at Pete for involving me, but I tried to dismiss the thought. The drive seemed both surreal and interminable. Eventually, I was dropped off at the door of an attractive private residence at the end of a dirt road and told that I would be spending the night there. I observed that the house was completely isolated from any neighbors, and I was informed that the psychiatric work there was essentially a covert operation.

I entered the front door and noticed a room off to the right side of the foyer. Inside was a twenty-four-year-old man wearing nothing but a huge diaper. I was jarred to see that he was strapped to a substantial, rugged wooden chair that reminded me of an electric chair. A friendly, obese man and his unusually tall wife approached me and introduced themselves as the caretakers. I asked them about the man in the chair, and they told me the story of Vinnie. He had been transferred from Birchfield Lodge, a private psychiatric facility. He was severely catatonic and could not be reached by anyone. On the occasions that he did come out of his trancelike state, he alternated between fits of rage and horrible, frightening nightmares. His psychotic dream life was one of eternal agony. Endowed with enormous strength and athletic ability, and manifesting extremely violent outbursts, he was rumored to have murdered a psychiatrist at the institution where he had been previously committed. His family had sent him to Rosen as a last resort because of the doctor's reputation for successfully treating difficult cases. So far, the attempt at treatment had not had the slightest impact.

Soon after my arrival, I witnessed Vinnie's rage firsthand: his body contorted, his face and eyes radiated pure hatred and, as he writhed around, the force of his savage movement seriously tested the integrity of the sturdy chair. The wood crunched and ground against the metal supports, stressing the materials near to a breaking point. Even for those of us in the next room, Vinnie's raging emotion was terrifying. The one night I spent in that house filled me with trepidation.

The next morning, I assisted the couple in washing Vinnie and changing his monstrous diaper. I noticed that Vinnie had an angry response and seemed to wake up a bit when the woman's arm accidentally brushed against his chest. I took note of the patient's reaction for later reference.

That afternoon, I was transferred to the home where I would work and where Louise, who would teach school in a nearby community, and I would reside. It was a remote, sprawling, country-style house. Its curved driveway fed off of a two-lane road that led up to a bridge crossing the Delaware River. The place was surrounded by a small forest. I was told that deer often grazed on the expanse of lawn in the mornings. The beautiful surroundings were breathtaking.

Around eleven o'clock that evening, Pete came over to visit with his wife, Jennifer, and their small daughter, and we enjoyed a happy reunion. They were living by themselves in town, and Pete worked with patients at several of the treatment residences. He would drive to each home on his rounds every day. At Rosen's request, Pete and I would function as co-therapists for the time being. I was glad to be working closely with Pete and was anxious to get started. It felt good to see a friendly, familiar face in this strange environment. We celebrated the occasion with a toast to our endeavor.

My new household was composed of Norm, a large, haunted man of Jewish descent who wore two large wooden crosses around his neck and had been transferred from New York State Hospital, a facility for the criminally insane near Albany; and Cynthia, a woman with a fixed gaze who had tried to kill her husband with a knife. Also living there full-time were Norm's sister, Carol, a young woman with big breasts who was lusted after by patients and therapists alike and who was there to look after her brother; and Vivian, an overbearing, intrusive psych assistant who was unpopular with everyone and was about to be fired. I couldn't wait for Louise to arrive to bring some semblance of normalcy to my living situation.

When I came on the scene, Pete's primary focus was on his work as a therapist with Norm, Cynthia, and an adolescent named Martin, who also lived in our house. The youth exhibited all of the polite and servile mannerisms of an Asian houseboy and identified himself as Chinese, despite his obvious white extraction. I assumed that his behavior reflected some form of psychotic delusion.

Previously Norm had tried to escape, and Pete had gotten into a fierce battle with him. It was an even match until Vivian rushed in to protect Pete and hit Norm over the head with a cast-iron frying pan. The blow had stunned the patient long enough for Vivian and Pete to get Norm into a straitjacket. By the time I arrived at Rosen's, it had become standard apparel for him.

Our house appeared like any other, except for the straitjackets, which the patients wore at night, on the clothesline and the wooden bars on Norm's window. The knives had to be locked up in a cupboard and were used only as needed, never casually left around. These and the many other necessary precautions that had to be taken heightened the tension of those of us who lived there.

I had never been around such overt violence and madness, and I was disconcerted, even frightened, by it. To compensate, in those first days I acted tough, demonstrated my athletic skill in the yard by throwing a baseball around, established a budding flirtation with Carol, and responded to Vivian's nastiness by throwing her bodily into the shower with her clothes on. These actions did not go unnoticed in the small community of caretakers, therapists, and patients. Within forty-eight hours of my arrival, I had become established as somewhat of a folk hero.

I began to get a feeling for the community I was living in: there was Rosen, the God figure; several tall, blond men and their wives—Peter being head guy; three graduate students in psychology; and a number of seriously mentally ill patients. Of course, Rosen functioned as the kingpin. Everyone stood up when he came into the room, but I refused to comply and would remain conspicuously seated. I could not participate in such an obvious buildup and adulation. For some inexplicable reason, there were no unpleasant repercussions for this blatant breach of protocol.

The Germanic types took care of all of the practical matters—they came to the rescue of therapists when there was danger of violence, constrained the patients as necessary, and took turns acting as bodyguards to Rosen. In general, these men treated me respectfully and politely, but I took issue with their occasional insensitive treatment of the patients. Per Rosen's orders, patients were disciplined, supposedly "for their own good," in order to make the overall situation more manageable.

The economics of the organization were of particular interest. Dr. Rosen was paid vast sums for his services, making him the highest paid psychiatrist in the country, if not the world. The patients came from the wealthiest families, people in high society with significant fame and fortune. Rosen charged a minimum of $20,000 to $30,000 a month for his unique treatment, which was a lot of money in those days, or even now for that matter. We, the stalwart therapists, were paid $75.00 a week over and above room and board, and we were happy to get it.

I had a busy work schedule. Pete and I would make the rounds each day, and we would treat virtually all of the patients, struggling to establish contact with them, interpreting the manifestations of their psychoses, and offering empathy and emotional support. We couldn't leave Norm and Cynthia unattended, so they accompanied us as we drove to the other houses. Pete and I worked hard and were tireless in our devotion.

I was grateful for my experience with Brodsky, and with another friend in Denver who suffered from painful auditory hallucinations. My time with them had an immediate carryover to these patients. I was surprised at my clarity and understanding of their problems and the probable sources of their torturous voices. My work was effective, and Rosen complimented me and wished me further success.

To my dismay, for the first few weeks the good doctor continually courted my approval by telling me stories of his remarkable cures in a boastful manner. I wanted to respond appropriately, but no matter how hard I tried, my praise always came out sounding condescending. Eventually, Rosen left me more or less on my own, and his visits to our household became rare.

Rosen was away on vacation when Pete and I started working closely with Vinnie. Our first problem was to get his attention. Up until then, no one had been able to rouse him from his apathy and withdrawn, dreamlike state. I remembered the reaction he had had to the caretaker that first day when she had inadvertently touched his chest. I thought it was significant. I suggested to Pete that we do the same, and he said, "What have we got to lose? Let's try it." Pete reached out and touched Vinnie's chest, and the heavily restrained man became instantaneously angry. He was highly agitated and began thrashing around in the wooden chair as best he could, given his constraints. We touched him again, and his anger increased to a fierce rage. Only this time I wasn't in the other room. Pete and I were right there beside him, and his reaction terrified us. Nevertheless, something significant had transpired during this angry outburst because Vinnie was beginning to make rudimentary contact with us.

Through all of this, I kept telling Vinnie in a calm, reassuring tone, that Pete and I wanted to help him come out of his frightening nightmare. We wanted him to feel better and we would take good care of him. We would give him good milk. Our meaning was both symbolic and literal; we actually offered him milk. I repeated these words and placed my hand on his shoulder. I felt sincere in my offer and was saddened by the plight of this tormented young man.

As the days wore on, there was the barest hint of recognition when we would approach Vinnie. He reminded me of a giant awakening from a deep sleep, who opens his eyes and eventually smiles. We were far from getting him to smile, but we no longer had to use devious means to begin to get his attention. We came every day and comforted him, and I was sure he was coming to know us. He would look at us, and he seemed to be calmed by our presence. We came to care a great deal about him, and on some level our affection was reaching him. We put our arms around his back and assured him that he was a good guy and that we loved him, all the while asking him to give up his fantasy of self-sufficiency, trust us, and accept a cup of milk.

After a few weeks, his mood was such that we released him from his constraints during our visits. He sat quietly with us and after a time began to answer our questions with a word or two. We took him to the bathroom to urinate, but he refused to use the toilet. He was holding onto his products at all costs. From fragments of conversation, we pieced together that his urine was symbolic of milk, and that he thought he could feed himself and keep himself alive. We told him that his mother's milk left him empty and had made him feel sick; we told him that's why he needed to make his own milk. He grasped that idea and repeated "made me sick, made me sick." We were kind and gently supportive as we continually offered the cup of milk. Then, one happy day, Vinnie accepted the cup Pete held out, and he drank the milk.

Pete and I hypothesized that our experiment and interpretations interfered with Vinnie's self-gratification through fantasy.

He first became angry at us, then when we made the appropriate interpretations and treated him with affection, he was able to rely on us for gratification. In a sense, our interpretations of his psychotic solution may have made the fantasy less rewarding, and our love and affection induced him to take a chance once again on object gratification. He gradually began to emerge from the schizophrenic process.

From that time forward there was noticeable improvement. Vinnie slept better, was nonviolent, and would converse with us in simple terms. We could free him and take him with us for rides. There was a basketball hoop outside in the driveway, and Vinnie, Pete, another attendant, and I would play two-on-two. Vinnie was still immobile and would just stand in one spot, distracted by voices, but if I threw him the ball, he would catch it instinctively and shoot it one-handed into the hoop from any angle. It was an amazing performance indicative of past skill and athletic prowess.

When Dr. Rosen came back from his trip, he heard about Vinnie's progress and went to pay him a visit. He found the young man unresponsive and sent for Pete and me.

"Say, I had the impression that you guys had really gotten someplace with Vinnie, but I don't see it," he jibed as we came through the door. But when we walked up, Vinnie clearly indicated that he recognized our presence, relaxed his rigid posture, and showed signs of life. We demonstrated that he was able to carry on a simple conversation with us.

We expected praise, but Rosen remained silent. Then, the next day, we received word that we were no longer required to work on the case. There was no explanation, just that those were Dr. Rosen's orders.

When we heard this news, we were completely thrown by it. It's difficult to explain our feelings to someone who hasn't worked closely with regressed patients. You develop deep compassion for them, and when they progress, these feelings intensify. It must be how a sensitive mother feels about her baby. That's the closest I can come to explaining it. It was a kind of agony to be wrenched away from a person we cared about so much. We weren't stupid, and we easily recognized that our beginning to reach Vinnie, where Rosen had completely failed, had wounded the doctor's vanity. This interpretation was no consolation to us, and we were left helpless and furious. We appealed our case, but to no avail. My disrespect and hatred for our supposed mentor increased exponentially. What had happened to the young Dr. Rosen who had shown such courage and dedication in working with disturbed patients? Some say he changed radically after an automobile accident that nearly cost him his life. For me, it was difficult to imagine that he had ever been any different.

The evening ritual at our house was that each night Louise and I would put our charges to bed. Cynthia felt more secure when she wore a straitjacket at night, so we tied it loosely, pulled up her covers, and kissed her good night. With Norm we took far more serious measures. His straitjacket was firmly fastened, and when he lay down on the bed, we placed a heavy restraining sheet over him. This thorough tie-down was Norm's nightly fare. To ensure even greater security, we placed other obstacles in his path toward freedom; Norm's clothes were kept in another room for the night, the door to his room was locked and bolted, and there were strong wooden bars on his window. Only Houdini could have escaped from this form of confinement.

One morning, when I came to release Norm, I was shocked to find that he was missing. The restraining sheet and straitjacket were carefully folded, the bed was made, and the wooden bars were neatly stacked in a corner of the room. We couldn't help being impressed with Norm's success as an escape artist, but it posed an awkward and frightening problem. Norm was a dangerous psychotic on the loose somewhere out there. He had to be located as fast as possible and returned to a secure environment, or somebody would get hurt. The search began immediately and everyone at the treatment center was involved. Rosen called a private detective agency, and our staff was sent around the area to see discretely if we could find anything out about Norm's whereabouts.

It was Pete who stumbled upon the first real clue. He overheard a man at the local gas station telling a strange tale about seeing an apparition the night before on a nearby bridge. He said that it looked like a huge man dressed only in a sheet, with two big crosses around his neck. He was swearing that he was "never gonna touch a drop of booze again," when Pete interrupted him to ask which way the apparition had been heading.

After about a week, the detectives finally located Norm in New York City, and the details of his escape were brought to light. After removing the bars, Norm had climbed down from the second floor wearing his two wooden crosses and carrying only a sheet. Because his clothes were in another room, Norm, either too polite or too afraid to wake anyone up, left without them. He walked along the road, crossed the bridge, and managed to hitch a ride into New York City, about seventy miles away. Norm was clever and explained to a gullible motorist that he had been camping in a field on the side of the road and somebody had robbed him and stolen his clothes. The motorist helped him get new clothes and dropped him off in downtown Manhattan. He actually got a job as an attendant at a city hospital and was working there at the time that he was found. Norm was returned, accompanied by two of Rosen's large attendants. They took him into a room and convinced him never to run away again. I was excluded from the confrontation and objected to what I imagined was probably harsh treatment, but the matter was officially dropped.

After Rosen's inappropriate and destructive responses in regard to both Vinnie and Norm, I began to wonder why I was continuing to work for him. Aside from the questionable behavior on the part of Rosen and his staff, living with disturbed patients on a daily basis was grueling at best. Then there was the added pressure of having to hide the fact that there were mental patients residing in the plush residential area of Bucks County. If this became known in the community, there would be serious consequences; if nothing else, property values would fall to an all-time low. So Louise and I were forced to live a kind of secret, underground life.

That was the least of it. Our routine lifestyle left us always on guard. For example, Norm, who was used to living in a straitjacket, had learned to turn the pages of a book with his tongue and, feeling sorry for the other residents, utilized this acquired skill to release dangerous patients from their restraints. Cynthia posed a different management problem. She had a proclivity to expose her vagina to the public, and she would display herself at the most inopportune times. One day Pete, and I were playing tennis in the city park while Norm and Cynthia sat on the sidelines. I glanced up from our game and was flabbergasted at the sight of Cynthia's legs spread wide apart, leaving her pubic region completely visible. From that time on, we made sure that our routine checklist before we went out included a panties check for Cynthia.

Maintaining social acceptability and safety in Dr. Rosen's bizarre surroundings required eternal vigilance. When I first got back to Denver, I was sitting at the kitchen table and started to feel a wave of anxiety and was dumbfounded as to its cause until I noticed that there was a large knife left out on the counter. Only weeks before, at Rosen's, that would have presented a serious threat.

While working under these unusual conditions, I felt strange and disoriented at times, and occasionally the tension carried over to my vacations. On a two-day trip to New York, I was walking in downtown Manhattan when I suffered from the illusion that the tall skyscrapers were falling in on me, and I felt like I was going to lose my balance. I was able to shake off the feeling, but it left me disconcerted.

Although my stay at Dr. Rosen's was sometimes painful and harrowing, I was determined to stick it out. However, in spite of my commitments, circumstances forced me to leave after a year and a few months. My military-draft exemption did not permit a prolonged absence from the university.

It was my good fortune that the time spent at Rosen's was considered by the psychology graduate department at Denver University to be an adequate substitute for the traditional internship requirement. The only remaining requisites for my PhD were the written dissertation and the final oral examination.

I had planned to submit my original formulations about schizophrenia as my thesis for the PhD, but there was a serious hitch. The standard research requirement included experimental design and statistics. My work was theoretical, and, as such, did not fit the acceptable framework. My advisor and good friend, Dr. Stuart Boyd, took up the cause with the rest of the faculty and argued that my work was a unique and worthwhile contribution. He told them that for this reason, traditional guidelines should be waived in my case. In addition, he pointed out that I had already demonstrated exceptional expertise in statistics and scientific methodology. Dr. Boyd's arguments prevailed over the objections of some of his colleagues, and my theoretical dissertation, "A Concept of the Schizophrenic Process," was decreed acceptable. I owed Stuart a major debt of appreciation for his efforts on my behalf.

Looking back at my experience with Dr. Rosen, I remember several reasons that caused me to regret my necessary departure. First, I was committed to the psychotic patients I was treating. I especially wanted the best for Norm and Cynthia. And, in addition to my caseload at Rosen's, I was also helping several young people therapeutically, who drove out from the city. They were artists and students, and I felt a special fondness for them. The thought of abandoning all of these people prematurely was unacceptable to me.

Second, Pete and I had organized and participated in a small therapy group, which included the two of us, our wives, and Jim Aldrich, a nervous and excitable graduate student in psychology from Yale. We were all learning a great deal about ourselves, and we were strongly motivated to continue.

The final reason was the most important of all: I was engrossed in a creative venture that was tantamount to an obsession. My mind was consumed by the attempt to unravel the riddle of psychopathology. My major point of concentration was the means by which those who were hurt or damaged attempted to defend themselves. If I could explain the mechanisms of defense that bent a person out of shape and accounted for various forms of mental aberration, and their causal relationship, I might have my finger on the pulse of a curative process.

I considered that mental illness was directly analogous to the physical malady of pneumonia; the body's defense against a threatening microorganism leads to fluid in the lungs, which can eventually become life-threatening. The body's defensive reaction is what does the most damage.

Schizophrenia, which was popularly thought of as a split personality, is the result of various combinations of biological predisposition and emotional trauma. Mental-health professionals are polarized in their approach, emphasizing one or the other aspect as more critical, and there is a legitimate difference of opinion. As a psychologist, I was essentially concerned with the mental component. I felt that problems of emotional maladjustment were similar to the situation in pneumonia in that they were determined not only by painful childhood events as causative agents, but even more so by how individuals defended themselves against the trauma they suffered. In all forms of psychopathology, the same defenses that originally sustained the hurt child adversely affected the adult in later life.

I observed that in the historical development of schizophrenic patients, their primary defense was a retreat into fantasy. When things got too rough for these people, they chose to retreat from real life and to live in their imaginations. They became excessively dependent on fantasy, which acted like a drug. The more they were addicted to imagining, the more they became dysfunctional, and the worse things got. In a manner similar to those who exhibit chemical dependency, they were involved in a downward spiral that ruined their lives.

I was stimulated by my growing insight and engrossed in the process of tracking down the mystery of mental disorder. In what way did fantasy compensate for the hurt and frustration experienced during the formative years? How did it come to be preferred over real gratification, and how and why did that work?

I hypothesized that fantasy gratification partially fulfilled the child's needs and reduced tension when there was deprivation in early life circumstances. If adequate parenting, particularly mothering, were unavailable, the child would form a fantasy bond or an imagined love or connection to the parent in order to compensate for any emotional deprivation. The more the child was hurt, the more he or she relied on this defensive retreat, which led to progressive maladaptation. The sense of merged identity fostered a feeling of pseudo-independence, that is, a feeling like, "I don't need anyone, I can take care of myself." Nevertheless, the person became more helpless and inadequate to cope with real circumstances, and he was left at the mercy of "voices," which he experienced as auditory hallucinations rather than as the self-deprecating thoughts that are also present in the "normal" and neurotic person.

In the final phases of the schizophrenic regression, however, these internal self-attacks, which are the sources of the patient's self-hatred, are disowned by the self and projected onto the outside world. Psychotic patients, in imagining that others hate them and accuse them, similarly imagine that they hear voices degrading them or ordering them to perform self-destructive acts. These hallucinated voices may be heard as commands to perform certain actions or as nasty comments shaming them. I noticed that often the voices reminded me of parental reprimands or orders.

The schizophrenic reaction could be conceived of as the end result of over-reliance on these defense mechanisms. The excessive dependency on fantasy gratification led to an inability to function in society, and the person eventually required hospitalization or some form of outside care in order to survive.

My thoughts were going wild with the implications suggested by this understanding. I became aware of the fact that the relationship between childhood pain and compensatory fantasy gratification applied to the neurotic as well as to the schizophrenic; in fact, it applied to everyone.

I enlarged my concept of defense formation while working with people in New Hope, in New York, and in the small therapy group with my associates and friends. These insights had obvious ramifications for all of us. Pete and I were quick to connect the concept of merged identity and the resultant illusion of self-sufficiency to developments in our own lives. We could see how our psychological defenses and pseudo-independent attitudes complicated and caused damage in our personal relationships. There was a rash of insights that expanded both Pete's and my understanding of personality dynamics, and significantly impacted our work.

Much later, I expanded the concept of the fantasy bond as a psychological survival mechanism to explain people's overidentification with family members, neighborhood, country, political systems, religious ideologies, and a host of other isms, such as capitalism, nationalism, and communism. These affiliations reduce our fear, offer a sense of security, and often lead to feelings of superiority toward people with different belief systems. They comfort us and make us feel less alone, but they polarize us against "outsiders."

People fight desperately to preserve fantasies that alleviate their anxiety and give them a semblance of peace. They react with hostility whenever their fantasy connections are challenged, and they lash out at others of different persuasions. Ethnic strife and religious wars spring from this source. Tensions are aroused when there are differences between one group's immortality project and defenses against death anxiety and those efforts of another. People act on the mistaken premise that the other must be subdued or destroyed in order for them to maintain a sense of safety.

These and many other considerations were rapidly surfacing in my hyperactive state of mind. I have never experienced anything like it before or since. My brain was racing from one idea to the next, and pieces of the puzzle kept falling into place. One insight led to the next and the next. It was a frantic but joyful time; the days flowed into one another, and I enjoyed a sense of exaltation. No other emotion compares with the feelings invested in this kind of creative inquiry. There is a state of rapture and enchantment that accompanies the thrill of discovery. I felt like I had found a secret that could possibly lead to a meaningful contribution in the field of psychology. Moreover, my theory carried implications that helped me to better understand myself and the people closest to me.

It's unlikely that I would have developed these ideas in my early twenties, or maybe at all, were it not for the unique atmosphere and circumstances of my time working under the auspices of Dr. Rosen. He offered me the privilege of engaging at close quarters with a number of severely regressed patients, which left an indelible mark on my overall career as a psychotherapist. It was not just a chance to hone my therapeutic skills, as I initially expected. In his book *Direct Analysis*, Rosen suggested preliminary hypotheses that applied Freudian theory and methodology to the treatment of the psychoses, and this approach eventually affected aspects of my own theorizing.

For example, we both emphasize the significance of the oral period (the first year and a half of life) in shaping the psychological future of the individual. In regard to methodology, we both stress the importance of exposing and challenging deep-seated, self-limiting defenses in a more or less open and direct manner in order to facilitate the maximum development of the individual.

Dr. Rosen presented a true dilemma for me. Whereas I admired him for his germinal contribution to the field as a therapist and free-thinker, I despised him for his autocratic manner, his vanity and showmanship, and at times his punitive, disrespectful attitude toward both patients and therapists. But more than any other emotion that I feel when I think back to those days is my deep gratitude for the entire experience.

AUTHOR'S NOTE

It is important to reiterate what I said earlier regarding the etiology of schizophrenia, that one must consider the biological predispositions as well as the underlying psychodynamics. Although my work focuses on the psychological and emotional issues in child development, it does not deny or minimize other powerful influences on the psyche of the child. Biological tendencies, inherited temperamental differences, and physiological predispositions combine with personal environmental influences to form unique and complex phenomena. There is no single cause of specific symptoms or mental aberrations. All psychological functions are multi-determined. Indeed, recent studies have demonstrated how both genetic *and* environmental factors contribute to the development of schizophrenia in adolescents and young adults.[2]

CHAPTER 8

REGRESSION

I was having a quiet dinner with my wife and friends at Jade West in Century City when I received a phone call from my answering service. I was informed that a client of mine was in the hospital at UCLA Medical Center and for further information I needed to contact a person named Samuel Jones at a number the answering service gave me. I was immediately anxious, not knowing what or whom the call referred to. I called Jones right away and when he picked up, he informed me that he had a Jamie Jenson in the Intensive Care Unit. She had attempted to take her own life and was in critical condition. I asked how he had found me, and he told me, that Jamie had had a piece of paper with my name on it in her possession when the paramedics picked her up. He asked about me about my relationship to her, and I told him that I was her psychologist. He said, "Well, something must not have gone right."

I thought to myself, "What an asshole!" I jumped in my car and headed at high speed toward the hospital. My heart was beating like crazy. On the drive, I thought about my talks with Jamie and pictured her sitting across from me. She was a tall, young woman in her early thirties, with long curly hair. Her manner was gentle and appealing.

Finally I arrived, found the ICU, and was allowed to enter. When I approached her cubicle, I saw a body huddled on one side of the bed. From where I stood, there was no sign of breathing or life, and I assumed that Jamie had just passed away. I felt an intense, all-consuming anguish over the loss. I also felt fear. This was the lowest point of my entire career as a psychotherapist. I had never lost a patient to suicide before, and I was afraid of any potential legal consequences. Every therapist is afraid of these consequences. I was in agony.

A minute later, I found out that she was still alive, but just barely. I left the hospital feeling only a minor semblance of relief. Although I was not religious, all that night I prayed that she would live.

The next morning, I was told that Jamie had survived and was medically sound. I felt a rush of relief and happiness. I headed for the hospital and found her lying in bed, looking fatigued but otherwise all right. She even managed to smile at me for a moment. She said that she felt so sorry for what she had done. I comforted her and assured her that we were going to work hard in order for her to feel better.

Later in the day, Jamie told me the details of her evening. She had left her apartment at about four in the afternoon with the plan of killing herself. She checked into a room at the Beverly Crest Hotel and then ordered and consumed a huge meal of fried chicken, mashed potatoes, lots of bread, and a large slice of cherry pie. She had been systematically collecting pills for a long time and had a lethal dose of tranquilizers, barbiturates, and diazepam in her possession. After eating, she ingested the pills and started feeling drowsy. She told me that at the last moment of consciousness, she had one clear thought: "Wait a minute. This is working. I don't really want to die." Then she did two things: she wrote my name on a piece of paper and she called UCLA hospital. Fortunately, she remembered the phone number from having worked there several years before. The operator connected her to the emergency room of the hospital, and Jamie managed to tell them that she needed help and where she was located. The hotel was nearby, enabling an unusually rapid response. The doctors told me that if her stomach hadn't been so full of food, she would certainly have died.

A few days later, Jamie was released from the hospital and returned home. She was shaken up but in good shape otherwise.

We continued our sessions and maintained daily contact. She promised me that she would never do anything that self-destructive again.

In thinking about Jamie's suicide attempt, I questioned myself about where things had gone wrong. It had been less than two months since she had come back to me for therapy. When she had called, I recognized her voice despite the fact that it had been several years since she had terminated therapy. At that point in her life, when she had concluded her first treatment with me—a combination of in-depth analysis and at critical times, voice therapy—she had been feeling good; her mood had been cheerful, she had been excited and deeply in love. In contrast, when she greeted me on the phone, her speech rhythm was slow and deliberate, and I had felt certain that she was depressed. After reintroducing herself, she was quick to mention that she wasn't doing that well and hoped that she could come in to see me again. I felt saddened by her call and, recognizing her sense of urgency, I arranged an appointment for the next morning. It took some amount of juggling to fit her into my schedule that day.

After Jamie's phone call, I thought a lot about her. She was intelligent and perceptive, and I had been fond of her as a client. When she had first come to see me many years before, she had appeared lost; she was about twenty-three or twenty-four years old, but she was very childlike and deeply immersed in fantasy. Years later, after a good deal of hard work on her part, she had emerged as an independent adult with bright prospects.

Two significant aspects about Jamie's childhood stood out in her case history. Her mother, Ruth, was a depressed woman who was extremely negligent. Given the circumstances, Jamie was basically forced to raise herself. Her father was weak and intimidated by his wife and had focused his sexual interest on the helpless child. He would coax her into lying with him in bed on Sunday mornings to read the comics. On these occasions, he would touch her inappropriately and rub up against her. Although he had always been the more nurturing parent, in the end this caused Jamie to feel betrayed by him. She was left feeling ambivalent in relation to her father—on the one side, affectionate and appreciative; and on the other side, guilty and hating.

Her mother was not only unhappy but also often threatened to kill herself. To my knowledge, she had never made an actual attempt. Yet, when she complained about her life and acted moribund, the other family members catered to her every whim, and in this way she maintained complete control of them. Jamie felt guilty to be happy and alive in that toxic atmosphere. Ruth's failure to thrive acted as an insurmountable barrier to her daughter's personal and sexual development. Jamie was slow to develop her femininity and had little sexual experience before meeting her boyfriend, Hal, six years prior to when I first met her. Hal was tall, strongly built, sensitive, and loving. From the start, they had a close and exciting sexual relationship. It turned out to be an ideal match, and the couple adored each other. From Jamie's standpoint, it was almost too good to be true.

However, from a conventional point of view, there was an obvious flaw in the situation. Hal was married. He valued the relationship with his wife, but they had grown increasingly distant over the years. They were still trying to work things out, but Hal wasn't particularly optimistic about their future and feared that their twelve-year relationship was in its last stages.

Nevertheless, this complicated set of circumstances had in no way dampened Jamie and Hal's enthusiasm for each other. They were both freewheeling individuals. They saw each other virtually every day and made love frequently, and neither had ever before experienced the depth of loving and being loved that they shared. They were truly happy, and that was where we had left off when I had last seen Jamie in therapy.

When I opened my waiting-room door the morning after her phone call, I was shocked to see that Jamie had gained a lot of weight, and there was little trace of the attractive, self-possessed young woman I had known before. She greeted me with a faint smile, but it was short-lived. She could barely contain her sadness. The moment we entered the consulting room, she cried full out. I asked her what was wrong, and she began to talk.

"Dr. Firestone, you remember when I last saw you, I was feeling really good. Well, now things are completely different; my life is miserable. I feel bad all the time. I even hate waking up."

"I'm sorry that you're feeling bad. Let's find out what happened to change things."

"I don't know where to start. Well, you remember my boyfriend, Hal, don't you?"

"Sure."

"He was irresistible to me. And so was my life and waking up each morning. In my most secret longings and daydreams, I never imagined a love like that. I loved looking into his eyes; I loved his face. He loved me, too."

"About a year after I left therapy, he told me how much he loved me and that he and his wife were getting a divorce. But instead of feeling overjoyed, I felt scared. I said all the right things about how happy I was and all that, but inside me it was different. That could've been the turning point . . . "

For a moment, Jamie sat there, staring blankly at the wall. She seemed void of all emotion. I asked, "What happened then?"

"It didn't happen all at once, but over a long time. I feel like I began to systematically destroy our simple, sweet relationship. I got crazy jealous when there was not even anyone to be jealous of. I felt angry and rejected when he would spend time with other friends, even male friends. I played on his guilt by acting sullen and pouting. I started to want to *make* him love me instead of *letting* him love me. I completely ignored what I was getting from him and focused on anything I wasn't getting. I nagged him all the time, and finally he started to get angry. Then we began to fight and by now he wants as little to do with me as possible, at least in any serious way.

"Hal still has some feeling for me, for a while we still saw each other and even had sex at times. But then he started dating other women. The worst thing is that now he's become pretty involved with another woman and they are always together.

"The woman was a distant friend of mine and I used to like her, but now I hate her. I fantasize about all kinds of terrible things happening to her. I'm ashamed, but I wish that she would die. I have cynical thoughts toward other people, too. Nowadays, I feel hateful all of the time, and like I'm bad, really bad. Sometimes, I even wish that I was dead."

I was alarmed by her last statement and said, "I can see that you are hurting a lot. When did you start feeling so depressed that you felt the need to call me?"

"It's been really bad for a couple of months, but it's getting worse."

"I'm sorry about what you are going through. I feel like you've been turning the anger that you have toward Hal and his girlfriend inward. You're feeling so guilty about your negative thoughts that you end up attacking yourself. That's what I believe is one of the causes of your depression. I hope that you can get the anger out in your sessions with me. I'm sure that will help you to feel better."

As we talked, our conversation seemed to temporarily lift her spirits.

Still feeling somewhat worried, I said, "Let's schedule three sessions a week, starting Friday. Meanwhile, keep in touch and if you feel particularly depressed or self-attacking, please give me a call."

When Jamie left the room, I felt a lingering apprehension about her state of mind. I hoped that she would accept my suggestion to call if she started to feel worse. I kept wondering about the cause of her regression. I thought that she was probably right when she said that it all seemed to go bad when Hal had decided to get divorced. That's when she started to provoke his rejection.

People are quick to account for setbacks in terms of negative events, but in this case my guess was that it was due to something positive. It seemed to me that Jamie was terrified at the prospect of a committed love relationship and a happy future.

I thought about how difficult it is to predict which situation will cause a pivotal emotional crisis for an individual. I knew that a uniquely positive acknowledgment is more likely to precipitate a person's regression when they have made significant progress in their personal development. I had often encountered this phenomenon in my practice and thought that it would make an interesting research project.

For almost two years before Jamie had become frightened in this way, she had enjoyed a rewarding relationship with Hal. Everything appeared to be stable, but I conjectured that at some point she realized how different her new life was from her past, and this is what made her anxious. The radical change in her self-concept and personal identity was so threatening that it altered the course of her life and there was a downward spiral.

As suggested, Jamie kept in close contact and regularly attended her 9: 00 a.m. sessions on Monday, Wednesday, and Friday. She mostly wanted to talk about her past relationship with Hal and dwelled on her symptoms of depression. I could not get her to freely express her anger. There were long periods when she was quiet and unresponsive, and she remained lethargic. She began to complain that the therapy was not working, and silently I agreed with her.

I encouraged her to participate in lively activities with her friends, to exercise, and to avoid isolation, but she was becoming progressively more inward. She began to have fewer and fewer exchanges with people, avoiding interactions, neither giving to nor taking from others. Isolation was her worst enemy, but she was stubbornly drawn to it. She cut off her feelings by eating, watching movies, driving around aimlessly in her car, and taking sleeping pills at night. These behaviors had become addictive. For example, if she felt particularly anxious or agitated, eating compulsively by herself or engaging in these other activities acted as painkillers. The eating accounted for her weight gain, and she despised herself for being fat. When questioned about when these patterns had begun to emerge, she dated their origin to the time that Hal had split with his wife and was completely available to her. Jamie's negative response to the good news had triggered a pattern of withholding, provoking, and retreating from Hal. This was the beginning of the tragic decline in their relationship and in her overall psychological well-being.

In listening to Jamie, I was reminded of a journal article I had written where I had defined withholding as a core defense utilized to create distance in personal relationships. When people hold back positive responses of affection, sexuality, shared activities, and kindnesses in relationships, it leads to progressive alienation.

Often people become afraid when they realize they are uniquely valued, loved, or respected. They fear any potential loss of the new situation. At first they may even have a positive reaction to their good fortune, but at a certain point the circumstances tend to trigger a person's latent death anxiety. Being especially prized makes life more precious, and the prospect of eventual loss becomes that much more painful, even agonizing.

The negative withholding reaction, which is usually unconscious, involves a gradual withdrawal from activities that were the most satisfying to them and most valued by their partners. Rationalizations are utilized to deny what is actually happening.

In general, the recipients of the withholding pattern become hurt, angry, and emotionally hungry, craving for what is missing.

Often people who become withholding find fault with others and blame them for their distancing behavior. Frequently they are turned against the same people whom they once regarded highly and loved the most, people who supported their best interests and personal goals.

Jamie's regression fit the exact pattern described above. In effect, she gave up the man she loved by holding back her most desirable traits and substituting unpleasant distancing behaviors. At the same time, she became depressed, sought isolation, and became addicted to food and increasingly self-destructive.

After a number of weeks, it was apparent that Jamie had done little to alter her regressed state of mind. But one morning she came to her session seeming excited, even a bit cheerful. She had the idea that it might help her to try to write a letter to her parents and tell them her story.

It sounded reasonable; nothing else was working, so I encouraged her to write them.

Dear Mom and Dad,

It feels difficult to begin this letter, yet I also feel eager to write it. It's hard to believe that I've been living in Los Angeles for almost ten years now.

When I asked you to come visit me several months ago, it was with the hope of finding out something about myself and about the years that we lived as a family in the house on Flagler Street. However, as I was waiting for your answer to my invitation, I realized that you could probably tell me very little of what went on with me during those 18 years. I feel sad to realize that you knew so little of what was happening within me, just as I knew so little of what was going on with you both or with my sister, Abby.

Whenever I picture the four of us living in that house, I always have the same image: each of us by ourselves, alone in a separate room of the house. Whether or not that is accurate, that is how it felt to me then and that is how I remember it now.

My recollection is that during those 18 years, I said very little about myself to you. The truth is that I said very little to anybody. I never talked to anyone, really, until I began therapy.

My experience of you, Mom, was one of total neglect. I have no idea what you were always so busy with, but it rarely, if ever, included me. I remember that you had a friend, Hannah, who you had known since the third grade. The two of you seemed inseparable. I hated her. Maybe I was jealous of her because it was so obvious that you preferred her company to mine, or to anyone else's in the family, for that matter. Years later, Dad told me that he didn't care very much for her. I think that he was being kind in choosing those words.

I remember that you spent hours cleaning the house. It was always spotless. You cared a lot about the condition of the house, but not very much about the condition of the people living in it.

I spent hours alone in that house. After a while, I began to enjoy my solitude. I came to prefer it to being anywhere around the three of you.

Our house seems so barren, when I think back to those years. There was so little nice feeling for ourselves or for each other. Mostly, I remember the fighting and anger and hatred between you two and the same between Abby and me.

One aspect of living that seemed almost totally absent from my childhood memories is anything to do with normal sexuality. I never knew much about sex until I was almost in college. I never found any evidence of it in our house. I remember the two of you almost always going to bed at different times. And your bedroom door was always open. In my 18 years of living on Flagler Street, in all of my wanderings in and out of drawers and closets and pocketbooks and everything else, I never found anything that even suggested anything sexual. Maybe it was very well hidden, or else maybe there wasn't anything to hide.

Whatever the truth is about these things, I do know that during my entire first year of therapy, I could barely even say the word "sex." I was too embarrassed to even say the word, much less connect to it in any real way. It took me many painful years to begin to live and see and feel about myself as a responsive, desirable, wanting sexual woman.

One subject along these lines that I did deal with in therapy had to do with you, Dad. I feel reluctant to write about this part of my life, protective of you. I hope that you will take it simply, just for what it is and no more. I remembered the times, usually on Sunday mornings, when I would come into your bed with you, and sometimes Abby, too, to read the Sunday comics. When I picture that scene, I remember Mom already conveniently downstairs, cooking breakfast. I remember being sort of curled up on my side with you curled up behind me. I have no other concrete memory of anything more than that. But I have a strong sense of something sexual about that contact with you, something inappropriate. And the tickling, too, that seemed to last a little too long.

I know that I partly liked these activities because there was such an absence of any physical touching in our family that whatever I could get, I wanted. I kept coming to you when you called me into your room on Sundays, and sometimes you even got into my bed with me—almost until I was 12. I felt both drawn to you because the physical touch felt nice and also repulsed because of the guilt I felt. In a way, it was natural for us to have those kinds of feelings toward each other. You were the only man I was around for many years. It was a pleasant experience, but it was also torturous. I was in such conflict about it. What you couldn't or wouldn't get from Mom, you tried to get from your children.

I remember having feelings of wanting to be nice to you because I saw Mom not being that way. I was confused by how rejecting she was of you, especially with affection. Sometimes I was even angry at her for being so ignoring of you. I thought that I would have been much nicer to you. Looking back, I feel sorry that you both missed out on what could have been a nice part of your life together.

With a man in my life, I have re-created that feeling of being left out. I have been drawn to that situation even though in reality, it feels horrendous. It has been a struggle for me to stop repeating my past with people in my current life.

In the summer, when our family came out to Los Angeles for a vacation, I had every intention of returning home in the fall. When I think back to that time, I still am not very clear about what in me made me not want to go back home. What I do know is that on some deeply unconscious level, the single requirement that might guarantee my chance to survive as an adult was that I not return home. Whatever small percent of me wanted to survive then really did, perhaps literally, save my life. I was so confused because at the time, I didn't know why I was doing what I was doing. It was the first strong, independent, brave move I had ever made in my life.

Well, that's my story. I hope that you will use it to understand me and why I left. I have tried to tell the truth, but always know that I love you. Please write me back about my letter as soon as possible, it's very important to me.

Jamie showed me the letter that she sent, and she talked about her feelings writing it: "At first, I wasn't even sure that I was going to actually send it to them. I just wanted to go through the process of what I would say to them, if I chose to. I would write some, then stop for a while, then an hour later I would pick it up again. When I finished, I was happy with what I had written. It was an honest recounting of what I had learned about myself. I wasn't writing this to blame my parents. Instead I thought that it would answer the many questions they probably still had about me, especially about why I decided to move three thousand miles away from home and never returned from what was supposed to be a two-week family vacation. So I decided to send them the letter exactly as I had written it, with not one bit of editing. I was so silly, I saw it as an offering, the most personal and meaningful gift I could give them."

After sending the letter, a couple of weeks went by without Jamie getting any sort of response. As the days passed, she felt more and more depressed. She became distraught from her parents' lack of response and thought that she had done something terribly wrong by writing to them. In our subsequent sessions, she was stubborn and barely spoke at all. When she did talk, she was critical of herself and felt that she was a bad person. She stressed the fact that she didn't deserve to live.

By that time, I realized that I had made a big mistake by not cautioning her about the communication with her family. Worse yet, I had supported the idea. I felt increasingly frustrated with her lack of progress and was worried about her self-destructive thoughts. Should I make arrangements for Jamie to be hospitalized? I went back and forth about the idea, still hoping that I could get to her, but obviously I was wrong. Then came that dreadful night when she barely survived her suicide attempt.

After Jamie was released from the hospital, she was awkward and nervous, but she was considerably less self-destructive and much more open and communicative in her sessions. She said that she was certain that she would never do anything to harm herself again. She and I both knew that the continuing therapy experience would be difficult and that it would require significant effort on both of our parts. After all that she had gone through, Jamie was very determined to improve her situation. She began by talking about her feelings prior to the suicide attempt.

"Not all of a sudden, but gradually over a period of time, my whole point of view changed. I hated myself and everything about me. I heard people saying critical things to me even when they weren't being critical. I became very cynical. It's like my whole way of seeing things switched. I became so negative and hateful toward other people in a way that I knew I didn't really feel. I couldn't understand where it was coming from. It was like I was superimposing an old way of being that absolutely did not fit onto my current situation."

Jamie had vicious "voices" telling her negative things about herself. They attacked her, saying that she was ugly and fat, that she had lost all of her friends, and that everyone hated her and that she should stay away from people. Lastly, they told her that "death was the only peace."

In our sessions, she was able to discover the origin of these hateful thoughts. She associated them with a general feeling she had had as a child that she was basically unlovable. In other words, she had adjusted her new situation to fit her core self-concept that she was worthless.

By utilizing voice-therapy techniques and saying her negative thoughts in a dialogue format, understanding their origin and answering back, she was gradually able to reprogram her brain and establish a more positive outlook. Furthermore, expressing the sadness associated with her childhood pain gave her a welcome sense of relief.

The biggest difficulty that Jamie faced was attempting to break with her inward addictive patterns of isolation and compulsive eating. Challenging these habits required a considerable amount of self-discipline, but over the next few months, she persevered, gradually regained her good figure, and began enjoying a normal social life.

In addition, she also had to cope with her stubborn pattern of withholding. Slowly she began dating, met many different men, and, finally, fell in love again. That was the most significant challenge given the negative reaction she had had to Hal's choosing her.

In that regard, we worked on a deeper understanding of what had happened in her relationship with Hal. She became aware of the fact that his love and respect for her conflicted with the basic negative identity she had formed in her family, and it disrupted her psychological equilibrium. Throughout her childhood, she had held onto the belief that she would never be chosen. This core feeling was threatened when Hal told her that he was getting divorced and wanted to spend his life with her.

These insights and the accompanying emotional catharsis helped Jamie to progress. She regained her sense of aliveness and good feeling, and, a year later, terminated therapy.

Generally, individuals who have attempted suicide are not amenable to being interviewed after recovery. Thus, there is a lack of direct, personal communication with people who might offer insight into suicidal ideation and behavior. My desire was to conduct a research study to shed light on the phenomenon and reveal its underlying secrets. Therefore, twenty years after the fact, I had the idea of trying to contact Jamie and to ask her if she would agree to be interviewed.

It had been so long since we had seen one another that it was difficult to track her down, but I finally succeeded in locating her. I was apprehensive when I called, wondering what had become of her, and hoping for the best. When she answered the telephone, her voice was bright and energetic. She was surprised but happy to hear from me and very sweet in our conversation. She told me that she had married years ago and that she had two children, and she especially wanted me to know that she valued her life. She told me how grateful she was for the time we had spent together, and how much it had helped her have the life she had now. She had a positive response to my request for an interview.

When we met, she looked pretty and composed, and again she expressed sincere appreciation for my help. She had a genuine desire to pass on any information that would be valuable in order to be of help to others. I was touched by her kindness and desire to pay back, because I knew that being reminded of those terrible times would be very painful.

As Jamie's interview unfolded, she referred to a pattern of thoughts that almost completely dominated her thinking during that period of her life. Below I will attempt to summarize the substance of her dialogue with me about her suicidal thought process.

Jamie: I tried to cut myself off from any feelings—I didn't want anybody to get to me.

Dr. F: What did you tell yourself, in effect?

Jamie: *Don't let anybody see what's going on. Look okay. Smile, look normal.*

Dr. F: What thoughts did you think about yourself?

Jamie: I hated myself. I felt that I was bad. Like there was something really bad that I couldn't fix. I couldn't stand myself. That's what I couldn't live with.

Dr. F: What did you hate about yourself? What things?

Jamie: I never liked the way I looked. I couldn't look at myself. The way I felt took the form of: *You're so ugly. Who would chose you?*

The voice attacked Jamie's relationship by criticizing Hal and belittling her.

Jamie: My voices were: *You don't really like him. He doesn't matter that much to you. There are other people that he likes. There are other people important in his life.*

Eventually, her voices generalized these distorted views to include everyone in her interpersonal environment:

Jamie: *Don't be stupid, you're not that important. You don't matter to anybody. Who would care if you weren't around? People would miss you a little at the beginning, but who would really care?*

I tried to get alone because this process occurred when I was alone. The voice was weaker when I was around other people, so the voice got me to be alone, saying, *Get alone so you can think.*

I started to think things like, *If you don't matter, what does matter? Nothing matters. What are you waking up for? You know you hate waking up every morning. Why bother? It's so agonizing to wake up in the morning. Why bother doing it? Just end it. Just end it. Stop it!*

Jamie confided that thinking about these plans began to give her pleasure. She said that even then she was puzzled by the perversity of enjoying the rehearsal of her strategy for self-destruction.

> Jamie: At first, just thinking about the details was enough, but soon I had to actually make real plans. At the very end, close to the time where I really did start to kill myself, I would drive around and the voice would badger me, *Well, where are you going to do it? How are you going to do it? Where can you go? You have to go to a hotel.*
>
> Dr. F: Did you hear this voice as a hallucination—as if it were coming from outside yourself?
>
> Jamie: No. They weren't hallucinations. I didn't actually hear voices. These were thoughts I had, in my head. But clear thoughts. I would think, *When are you going to do it? Go ahead and do it, you coward! You're so cowardly. You can't even do this, can you? You better do it already, Just do it!* Finally I acted on my impulse, and you know the rest.

Jamie's thought processes coincided with what other suicidologists have described as a "suicidal trance state." In this state of mind, individuals prone to suicide become increasingly obsessed with a flood of critical and destructive thoughts about themselves and everything about their lives. Later their thoughts push for immediate destructive action.[1]

As Jamie revealed her secret thoughts, I was touched by her bravery and impressed with her compassion in sharing the most painful moments of her life. I felt a deep affection for her and an appreciation for her cooperation. But I was particularly happy that currently she was doing well and enjoying life.

CHAPTER 9

MR. MARKS

"Good morning, Mr. Marks. It's good to see you." I felt like I knew Jerry much better after what had turned out to be a remarkable group session the previous night. Jerry Marks was a thirty-nine-year-old engineer suffering from an obsessive-compulsive neurosis with paranoid tendencies. It was early April 1969, and my first session of the day. I was particularly interested in how the clients who had never before participated in group therapy had reacted to the new experience. I thought about the dramatic events of the previous evening and felt a renewed interest in my practice. How would the group process affect the participants in their individual sessions? Would it energize them and lead to significant breakthroughs? Would there be an upheaval in their interpersonal relationships?

"How did you feel after participating in the group?"

"Not that bad. You know, that was a hell of a session. I'm not kidding you."

"What do you mean?"

"Well, you know, everyone crying and letting go. I thought I was the only one like that. Jesus, I felt closer to those people than I ever felt before toward anyone." Jerry looked sad, and he paused. Then, as often happened, his thinking ran off in an entirely different direction.

"You know, Doc, you look cheery this morning. I envy you. I kept picking at myself last night, couldn't get to sleep listening to the people upstairs creaking the furniture—like they wanted to bother me, the smug bastards. I really hated them and wanted to kill them. What the fuck are they trying to do to me? And those bastards on the freeway yesterday, crawling along—and, you know something, I hate those cars that come up from behind you—you can't trust them—watch your exhaust pipe—maybe those cars are going to ram right into my rear end. Yeah, I know, Doc, that sounds real homosexual and paranoid."

"You know, you really sound like you're giving yourself the business this time."

I thought about when Jerry first came to see me. He interviewed me like I was a job applicant. Apparently, I passed the test—and then he attacked me for the next two years in practically every session. He criticized my looks, my office, my approach, my artifacts and, when he learned that I was Jewish, he attacked my fee structure. The funny thing is that his attacks never bothered me; I actually liked him a lot. When he settled down to work on his problems, he quickly learned the art of free association. That is, he learned to say everything he thought about or felt, without any of the usual considerations.

I turned my thoughts to Jerry's self-attacks, *What starts those feelings? God, this guy really punishes himself brutally every time he does anything good or right for himself. Those people upstairs and their noises—like parents watching him and focusing angry attention on his life. Still, everything centering on him.*

Jerry continued, "I really kick myself around, don't I?—I sure do—well, fuck you, Doc. You know, Margie is a good piece of ass, but she doesn't have an orgasm. Shit, I remember when I was really afraid for you to mention the subject of marriage, and I couldn't even think of it without terror. Hell, now I've been married for over a year, and it's really okay. You know, I really like having sex with her and it's been good lately. You know something, though? I think one of my balls is actually smaller than the other one. Look, I'm not kidding you, Doc, I think I'm going to have someone look at it—and my back's been hurting the last few days."

"You've really got everything wrong with you now that things are shaping up," I said. "Sex and fun must really be paid for. I wouldn't want to go too far with those good things. Better you should give yourself the shaft."

"You're pretty cute, Doc, but, really, I do feel happier lately, and I really like her—like I don't come home to a place by myself like before, and she's very nice to me. Sort of fooling around, teasing and wrestling, but she bugs me when she wants to talk about her day. Why do I freeze up and feel tense when she wants to talk? Shit, something happens to me. What's all this bullshit about communicating? Yeah, and what does she want? What is it that females want anyway?"

I waited for Jerry to elaborate. During the long pause in the conversation, I became involved in my own thoughts, *Reminds me of Louise, talking about her day teaching. It's hard to listen to her. Maybe I'm not really interested in her, outside of her relationship to me. Hell, I feel guilty about that. No ... wait a minute. I am interested in her life ... it's just that she doesn't really talk to me anymore about real things. She prattles on about insignificant subjects, gossips about other teachers, practical stuff about our kids. That really bothers me. Whatever happened to the interesting, pretty woman I fell in love with? When did she stop talking to me?*

I remembered a couple of weeks ago when we went away with the kids; we always seemed to be missing each other like "ships that pass in the night." We were always crossing paths. I'd be getting into the pool with the kids and she'd be getting into her bathing suit, then she would be coming into the pool just as I was getting ready to come out. I thought of making love, and she'd be reading. Then she'd come to bed and want to make love when I was falling asleep. I knew something bad and painful was happening.

Once again my thoughts returned to the session. Jerry was saying, "What is it women want? What do they want?"

"Just say your feelings—what are you thinking now?"

"I was just thinking that I do like Margie a lot and—"

"It looks like you're feeling something right now. Let it out."

"Shit, I'm starting to cry like a baby, Doc. Every time I start to feel good about something, like love or closeness, I get this feeling like I told you I get when I listen to Wagner. Like something breaks loose and this terrible sadness comes to me. Why do I come apart like this?"

"What does it make you think of or feel?"

"Yeah, I think of the bitch. That skinny, weird, bitch. Shit, she didn't have any love in her. What a turd—yeah, and sickly, always sickly—finally dead. Why was she always sick all the time?

"And the fuckin' old man—shit, he thought he was something, trying to sail around the world. Did I ever tell you? He put out to sea to sail right across the Atlantic Ocean in a twenty-eight-footer, but he got scared and turned around and came right home. Maybe he was afraid like me, the son of a bitch.

"And the goddamned sisters all over the place! All of them walking around like a peep show. You know, my sisters are really good-looking and I used to watch them undress. Sort of sneak up on them—made holes in the doors—wanted to see their pretty new tits and pubic hair. Sometimes they'd catch me and get me into trouble, and the fuckin' parents would say 'Leave them alone, Jerry,' or get really mad and kick the shit out of me. 'Jerry, go play with your marbles,' in a high falsetto. Shit.

"You know, I still go to those movies once in a while and masturbate. Those kids around sixteen or seventeen really turn me on—like on that teenage dance show on TV. Then I feel guilty as hell. When I come home, it's hard to look Margie in the face."

I felt sad as I listened to Jerry. *What a complicated, guilty existence*, I thought, *what emptiness. No wonder he cries. He sure has had a lot to work through: the emotional starvation—no strong father to identify with—the eerie, incestuous themes that were intensified by his hunger for love—enticed by his sisters and then punished for it.*

I remembered my own childhood. I knew what Jerry felt like. The sexual guilt I had felt. "Don't touch her there. How dare you? You're going to get it!" My mother, usually calm and sweet, turned into a monster and lashed out in a fit of rage because when I was five or six—before I really knew any better—I inappropriately touched my sister, and she had tattled. There had been real hell to pay.

This train of thought reminded me of the succession of live-in maids who stayed in the room next door to the one I shared with my grandfather. Especially Maria. As a child, I would lie on top of this pleasant, well-built country girl, fondling her large breasts. My penis felt tingling and excited, like I had to urinate. I was just a little kid, hoping that no one would see or hear anything, or I would really get in trouble.

Jerry continued, "You know, I don't masturbate much anymore, and if I slip, I don't feel so bad about it. I remember when I spent all my time alternating between shooting off my rocks and feeling weak and criminal. Like when I walked around with Margie at the beach and I was afraid guys were looking at us and that they'd attack us and I'd come out looking like a fool. Hey, you're right, Doc, I'm afraid, like you said, of retaliation for anything I do sexually—or even having a girl—like those guys will cut off my dick."

"Well, you have to be punished for all your sexual and competitive feelings. If no one else does it for you, you do it for yourself."

"Yeah and I'm pretty good at it, too. How long have I been coming to you, Doc?"

"It's been almost three years, but it doesn't seem like it."

"Well, I'm really glad I came to see you. Shit, I used to be afraid of everything and real suspicious. Remember that guy at work I was obsessed with—when you told me to read *Stern and the Kike Man*? I learned a lot about paranoia from that book. That was just like me in those days. I sure feel different now, and I'm really feeling like I like you, Doc."

"I'm glad you do," I felt warmly toward him and smiled. After glancing at the clock, I said, "I guess we have to stop today—I'll see you on Thursday."

I worked with Jerry Marks in biweekly individual sessions for approximately three and a half years. The primary treatment methodology was psychoanalytically based psychotherapy. My approach involved the utilization of free association, interpretation, and analysis, and the working through of transference reactions. In this form of talk therapy, the therapist acts as a blank screen, revealing as little as possible about him- or herself. Transference refers to the client's projections of feelings from their past onto the therapist.

In Jerry's case, his predominant feelings toward me were an angry representation of his feelings toward his father. They were appropriate emotional reactions to the severe criticism and hostility that he experienced while growing up. Because of my awareness of the source, I had little or no personal response to his rancorous outbursts. As time progressed, Jerry was able to separate these hostile thoughts and feelings out and to recognize that they did not apply to the current situation in therapy; and, more important, he learned to understand and regulate his anger in his life outside of my office. In the process, he became less fearful and more likable, which gradually improved his relationships.

When Jerry first came to me, he had had a deep-seated fear of other men. He projected his intensely competitive thoughts and feelings onto them, perceiving them as abnormally aggressive, even dangerous. He would cross the street if he imagined that he was being followed or if he saw a group of men standing and talking in front of a building. His paranoid beliefs and destructive voices made him acutely apprehensive and caused him a huge amount of grief on a daily basis.

As noted, Jerry's paranoia toward other men and toward me had its source in his feelings of anger toward his father. The circumstances in Jerry's childhood were such that he found himself in a "double bind" situation. While growing up, he could feel safe only when he denied his competitiveness and made himself appear less than his father in some way. At the same time, however, he felt enormous pressure to excel at school, which required assertiveness and a competitive spirit.

Jerry's father, a harsh authoritarian and a perfectionist, had imposed impossibly high standards on the boy. Jerry internalized his father's demands for perfection, and experienced hostile, self-critical voices whenever he fell short. In one session, Jerry revealed voice attacks that would make him incredibly tense and anxious when presenting data to his co-workers; *You'd better get this right, or don't say anything!* A small misstep would trigger another barrage of self-castigation. *See, you never get it right! You stupid, incompetent ass!*

As a small child, Jerry had to conceal any sign of the reactive rage he felt toward his father, otherwise there would have been dire consequences. In suppressing his feelings of anger and rage, he then projected them onto other men and anticipated retaliation and punishment from them.

Jerry had also been extremely distrustful of women. He had had few dates, and the majority failed to find him attractive. His reaction to women was directly related to his relationship with his mother, whom he characterized as rigid, cold, and indifferent. As he free-associated and understood the source of his cynical thoughts and maladjusted attitudes, he began to feel differently about the women he met, and they responded accordingly.

About a year after we began sessions, he met Margie, a sweet, pretty woman. They dated for a while and later the relationship became more serious. Jerry gradually overcame his fear of commitment and eventually proposed. Soon they were married, and a year or so later, they were thrilled with the birth of their son.

In the therapy group the night before, one of the participants, a beautiful actress, paid him a great compliment. She said that she found him attractive and liked his straightforward manner. Jerry could hardly believe that someone so good-looking would respond to him so warmly.

Whereas he had been initially somewhat retiring, fearful, and not particularly adventurous, as he progressed in therapy Jerry began to show a good deal more initiative in various areas of his life. He took up flying as a hobby and became a competent pilot.

Later, he applied for a job as an aerospace engineer at Cape Canaveral. He was hired and actively participated in the NASA space program during what turned out to be some of the most exciting years of space exploration.

When I was a graduate student in clinical psychology, I invested my time and energy in my own personal analysis with an experienced psychoanalyst. This endeavor opened up a new door to my self-understanding and insight. I was excited before each session and arrived early to contemplate my state of mind before I was called in. These talks became the central focus of my life at the time. The experience was not always pleasant; many painful feelings surfaced, and I had a lot of anger in my transference feelings toward my analyst. It was a difficult period for me, but I discovered a great deal, and I was impressed with the realization that there was no other conceivable means to have digested what I had learned in those sessions. As a result, I approached my work as a psychotherapist with a deep respect and dedication to the process, and a significant regard for my clients.

In effective psychotherapy, there is a strong emphasis on freedom of speech and the expression of feeling. For example, the method of free association used in psychoanalysis permits clients to let their thoughts flow in a stream of consciousness unhampered by the rules of logic or censorship. They not only learn to think creatively but also come to understand on an emotional level that any thought or feeling is acceptable. At the same time, they are taught to examine the consequences of their behavior in regard to their own best interests as well as in an overall moral perspective.

In the case of Mr. Marks, he was able to utilize the process of free association to reconnect to painful episodes in his developmental years and achieve insight into his current problems. This enabled him to challenge long-standing paranoid thoughts and debilitating defenses and to differentiate from a life that was not only limited but also extremely unhappy.

In my opinion, there is no experience that is comparable to offering a person the opportunity to think, talk, and feel openly, about his or her personal life. Aside from the curative aspect for those with special problems, the process of psychotherapy offers the maximum potential for clients to individuate, that is, to separate themselves from destructive programming, and lead a freer, fuller existence. As such, I would recommend an in-depth talk-therapy experience to any person seeking self-knowledge and personal growth, regardless of whether or not he or she suffers from emotional problems.

CHAPTER 10

FROM ONE SIDE OF THE COUCH TO THE OTHER

As I approached the door to my waiting room, I felt mildly apprehensive. The voice of the woman who had telephoned asking for an appointment sounded either deeply depressed or possibly psychotic. Her disaffected tone concerned me. I expected a grave interview and knew right away that I would have to make a diagnostic evaluation to determine the best course of action.

When I opened the door, I noticed that Linda had the appearance of a mentally challenged teenager. Although she looked to be fourteen or fifteen years old, in actuality she was in her early twenties. She was barely five feet tall and overweight; her hair was cut short in an unbecoming, severe style; and her eyes were dark and defiant. The awkward, tentative way that she walked as she accompanied me down the hallway to my office and her somewhat-rigid posture all contributed to a picture of strangeness and backwardness.

Once in my office, Linda sat stiffly in the chair opposite my desk. She was withdrawn and almost completely catatonic, barely responding to my standard questions about her history. Aside from sparse answers to the normal intake inquiries, there were virtually no responses. Near the end of the first session, Linda asked a couple of routine questions and then left, saying that she agreed to weekly sessions and would see me the following Tuesday. I felt pained by her condition, but almost immediately, I had a sense that I could be of help. There was something about Linda that intrigued me and inspired affection.

For almost a year, the same scene repeated itself week after week—fifty minutes spent in anticipatory silence. Linda always complied with the therapy regimen, arriving on schedule and paying on time, but she refused to communicate. She looked as if she wanted to speak but couldn't or wouldn't. Here was a young woman who had likely been stunted in her emotional development and possibly even in her physical growth by incidents in her formative years. But what had happened to her?

Although we had exchanged only a few words during the first twelve months of meeting, on a nonverbal level I believed a rapport was being established. In the hours of shared stillness, I felt a communion was taking place that I hoped would be setting the stage for a working therapy relationship. This was merely conjecture on my part, but as time passed with no observable change, I had my doubts.

I had a hard time during these preliminary sessions, because I had never worked with anyone like this before in my practice. I questioned whether I was doing the right thing for Linda by waiting it out. In the sessions, I was outwardly friendly and compassionate, but inside I felt increasingly anxious as the months passed.

Even though I felt awkward, while working with schizophrenic patients, I had acquired the necessary patience to deal with this type of impasse. One man in particular taxed me in this regard, and I learned the value of silence. With Linda, there were many nonverbal exchanges that took place which indicated that a positive bond was being formed. I began to care deeply about her, and I felt that she was beginning to trust me.

I talked to Linda about her silence, but at the same time, I respected her boundaries. I didn't push her to talk. I sensed that she had been severely intruded upon and that her stubborn refusal to speak had once been a survival mechanism. I surmised that she was sizing me up and would eventually become less guarded and speak more freely. Even though few words had passed between us, we were becoming comfortable with one another.

Linda began to mention a few things she noticed about me from time to time—the shoes I was wearing, the way my hands looked to her. Much later, she confessed that during her lengthy silence, it had been easy to talk about the shoes because, as she put it, "your shoes were inanimate and had no sexual connotation, but your hands were a different story." She remembered looking at my hands and said, "I didn't look at them as long as I wanted to because I was afraid that you would notice that I was staring at them. The truth was that I was wondering what it would feel like for you to touch me with your hands. The deeper truth was that I wanted you to touch me. It was a kind of a longing feeling."

It is relatively common for positive transference or even sexual feelings to arise in clients toward their therapist. What seemed unusual was that these feelings had come up so explicitly in someone so shy and introverted. I told her that I appreciated her openness. I thought to myself that her positive feelings toward me had been valuable for the therapy, because it was likely that they facilitated her trust in the process.

Slowly, cautiously, Linda also began to reveal bits of information about herself. She told me of her previous year at Cornell University, when she had sequestered herself in her dormitory room for two weeks, posting a sign on her door that simply read, "Go Away." This behavior had alarmed her roommates, who brought her food and eventually convinced her to get counseling. She took the advice, but the treatment proved to be of little real value.

Aside from these small pieces of information, she continued to remain silent for long periods, and I felt more and more uncomfortable with the way things were going. One day, after nearly a year had gone by, I made what, at the time, seemed to be a senseless and radical move that was a departure from my typically well-planned therapy approach. I walked over to Linda and picked her up, chair and all, and said, in a firm but benevolent tone of voice, "Linda, now you will speak. You must talk to me and now is the time. No more silence. That's all there is to it!" Somehow, even though *I* thought that my action was crazy, intrusive, and essentially disrespectful, Linda sensed that I was on her side.

Once she began to talk, she was full of surprises. Words poured out, and there was no stopping her. Linda disclosed that since the age of four or five, she had often considered suicide. These suicidal thoughts actually comforted her, and she frequently repeated to herself that "If I ever feel too awful, so bad that I can't stand it anymore, then I can always kill myself." She saw suicide as her only available escape, and she used its promise as a painkiller. When she disclosed this secret, she was not only embarrassed but also angry. She resented me, because revealing her intent to me weakened her resolve to do away with herself. She could no longer find as much satisfaction in thinking about this escape; in a subsequent session, she expressed her irritation.

"Sometimes I hate you, Dr. Firestone. Who do you think you are, anyway? You can't help me. Telling you about this just made me feel worse. Look, it's hopeless. What is there to live for anyhow?"

"Linda, I know that you're feeling hopeless. I can see that you are anxious from exposing your secret escape plan, but why not give it a try and hang in there? You can sweat through the anxiety. A lot of emotions are coming up from your childhood, and that can help you to feel better."

"But they feel so real. I'm not making them up!"

"I know that. They're uncomfortable, and sometimes they feel terrible. What I'm saying is that the intensity of your misery is not coming from experiences in your present-day life. Even though your pain feels very real, it is rooted in the torture of your past and is being projected onto your present adult life. What I'm saying is, hang in there. Try not to get ahead of yourself."

She seemed to calm down a little as she considered my words. Then, almost begrudgingly, she said, "Maybe I *could* feel different."

I nodded. "Therapy is for investigating thoughts and feelings, and looking into where they come from. Understanding this could help you a lot because it has to be different now since you are no longer a helpless child. As an adult, you can never be trapped like before. Present day, you can take power over your own life. Before, you were totally dependent on your family for survival. Now you are grown up and can take care of yourself."

In addition to Linda's suicidal proclivities, she also had violent impulses and felt as if she could commit murder.

"Almost every time I take the bus to my appointment with you, I'm so aware of these fat middle-aged women who pass me, walking down the aisle. I have such strong impulses to trip them— to just stick my foot out and watch them fall. I don't know why I think that. I don't even know them. They never did anything to me. But it's hard to stop the thoughts. Isn't that crazy?"

"What does that make you think?"

Linda looked confused and agitated, and she said, "I don't know what you mean."

"Just let your mind wander freely," I replied.

There was a tense moment before she spoke, "I just had a funny thought: I hate these women."

"You hate them?"

"Yeah! I really do!" She replied adamantly.

"'Hate' is a pretty strong word. What comes to your mind when you think of that word?"

Linda considered my question in silence. After a long pause, she muttered, "My mother, I guess. But you can't hate your own mother. It's not right."

"Right or wrong or whatever, feelings are feelings. You know, all feelings are okay. Only our actions can be bad. Does that make sense?"

Linda sat forward and became animated, "You know, she drove me crazy, always asking me questions about school, about everything, always prying. And sometimes she was just plain mean. I would never answer her stupid questions, and it drove her crazy. One day I remember coming home from school and she was crying. It was the only time I ever remember seeing that. When I asked her about it, she told me it was because I would never talk to her, never tell her anything. I remember feeling guilty to see her like that because I actually felt some sort of sadistic pleasure in seeing her hurt from something I did. I was ashamed that I considered it some kind of weird victory that had been years in the making. That's how I got even with her."

"That behavior might have been appropriate back then, but now being silent and withholding words is a serious detriment. It's just a carryover from your relationship with her."

"Yeah, she really got under my skin. Sometimes she was just a bitch. She'd get so angry, she would lose it and even hit me. I just had a memory of one time when I was standing in the bathroom next to her. I was eye level with the sink, so I must have been about four or five. All of a sudden, she just started hitting me in the face with her hand, over and over. She kept hitting me until she noticed that I was bleeding from what she was doing. She didn't stop until she saw the blood." Linda started crying softly, "I can't believe that I just remembered that."

"Let it all out," I said, and she broke down sobbing.

When Linda finally stopped crying, she told me that when her mother saw the blood, she was shocked and scared to see what she had done. Her mother begged for forgiveness, but this only confused Linda more. Linda said she had felt guilty, even though she was the victim of the attack.

In her next session, Linda spoke about the anger she felt toward her mother for the way she was treated as a child. "When I got to be about eight, I would walk home from school by myself. Every day I passed by the house of a girl named Gay. She was cute, with really curly red hair and freckles. I knew that she liked me because she would always come to my house and ask, 'Can Linda come out and play with me?' She seemed lonely and sort of sad. One day, I saw her in her front yard. She was smiling, glad to see me. For some reason, I don't know why, I walked up to her and I just started hitting her as hard as I could, and I didn't stop until she started crying. Then, I just walked away without saying a word. I've never understood that."

"What do you think it meant?"

"I really don't know."

"Just give yourself a minute to think about it."

"I don't know." She looked sad, "Maybe that little girl reminded me of me."

"Yeah that sounds right. But why hit her?"

"I guess that seeing her caused me pain for myself and I just couldn't stand it."

"That's an interesting interpretation. What does it make you think?"

"You know, Dr. Firestone, it's so strange—in my last session I told you about my mother beating me, and in this session, right away I thought about me hitting the little girl."

"In the first story, your mother was angry at you and I imagine that deep down you were angry back at her. Then in the next story, you acted out anger in the same way with the girl."

"I see, like I was punishing her like my mother punished me."

"Yes, she reminded you of yourself, and symbolically you were turning toward yourself the anger you felt toward your mother ."

"That's really interesting." Linda nodded her head, with a serious expression, as she took in the meaning of what I was saying.

"Think about it. You felt that it was unacceptable to be angry at your mother, so what else could you do but internalize it? But then sometimes it comes out toward others."

"I see what you are saying. You know, sometimes I feel like I'm a murderer. I have so much rage in me and I never know what to do with it. I've always been fascinated by stories about real killers. I read everything that I can about them. Mostly, I want to know what happened to them when they were growing up and what the thought process is that goes through their minds leading up to the time they kill. I've always thought that this morbid curiosity meant that I was crazy. I've been so ashamed and confused by these thoughts. I would tell myself that I was a horrible person, like *'You're such a monster! You're horrible. You're like a criminal. Nobody who's normal thinks these kinds of thoughts. You're a crazy person! You're crazy!'"*

At this point, Linda paused and looked at me expectantly. I guessed that she was concerned about what my reaction would be.

"It makes sense when you think about it. You were looking for insight into your rage. It's painful when you are bent out of shape by being made to feel hatred, especially toward those people you want to love. You know, Linda, I really feel that by identifying and expressing your self-hating thoughts, and by understanding your anger at your mother, rather than turning it against yourself, you can get to feeling better."

Linda seemed unusually relaxed toward the end of the session. She sat quietly for a while, but this silence had none of the resistance of our early meetings. She looked at me directly and smiled shyly.

"Thanks, Dr. Firestone, I feel so relieved and good from how our sessions are going."

Thinking back, I realize that I was especially aware of the close correlation between suicidal thoughts and thoughts that lead to violent behavior. Later, I would participate in research projects in this area and help develop scales to evaluate both internal and external forms of aggression. Prior to conducting this research, I had discovered that these tendencies are monitored by critical voices, which are internalized thought processes that are hostile or cynical toward both oneself and others. This realization helped me to better understand and cope with Linda's self-destructive and destructive preoccupations.

In one session, Linda described how she had come to live in California. At the end of her second year at Cornell, Linda had seized an opportunity to leave home and break loose from the stranglehold of her family, arranging, with her parents' approval, to visit her uncle in California. As her stay there was coming to an end, she was caught in a terrible dilemma. She could either go home or brave being completely on her own. The prospect of finding an apartment and a job and taking care of herself left her feeling frightened and alone. Nevertheless, she found a job at the United California Bank near UCLA and also enrolled in the college part-time. When she refused to return home, her parents were furious, but she held her ground.

As I listened, I admired Linda's courage and determination to struggle for her freedom. I was pleased that she was talking freely, and I felt considerable optimism about the course of her therapy.

She spoke more and more frankly about her childhood experiences and began to express powerful emotions and to identify other negative thoughts toward herself and other people. Her family claimed to be close and loving, but the truth was more the opposite. She was disturbed by the discrepancy between their loving words and insensitive, hostile actions. As a result, she was confused in her sense of reality. Prior to therapy, she had maintained a positive view about her parents while blaming herself for whatever had gone wrong.

As a child, Linda had been extremely overprotected and lied to about the realities of life and death. "Once, I heard the siren of an ambulance and I asked my mother what it was. She told me that an ambulance was something that took women to the hospital to have their babies. When I needed to have my tonsils out, I wasn't told anything about the operation. Instead, they woke me up early one morning and told me that I was going to visit my grandparents. The next thing I knew, I was in a hospital, with strangers doing all sorts of things to me, without even knowing why. I was screaming my head off when they wheeled me down the hallway."

Linda was intruded upon by her emotionally hungry mother, whose own needs were not met as a child. In a sense, she was trying to get *from* Linda the love she had missed in her own childhood. As a result, Linda was not only deprived of love, but her mother's fits of rage often led to the type of beatings Linda had described earlier. On one occasion, her mother had thrown her down a flight of stairs. Her father was judgmental and critical, yet on occasion tender and kind. She never knew what to expect in her home environment and had no real sense of safety. Her parents were never that close, were rarely affectionate, and appeared to be asexual. This was a crucial dynamic that inhibited Linda's overall development as a woman.

The only power that she had as a child was to go inward, become self-nurturing, and keep her thoughts and feelings to herself. In our sessions, she began to reverse this process. Linda's most formidable defenses had been to be withholding from her parents, and self-denying, which showed up in a mean, stubborn, isolated lifestyle.

Linda fought hard to dismantle these defenses during the course of therapy. Even though her neurosis had weakened her and caused her to become increasingly dysfunctional as she grew older, she somehow retained both a sense of what had happened to her as well as a powerful empathy for others. Underneath her character armor, Linda was able to preserve a nature of pure honesty and integrity that was rare.

Information kept pouring out of her, and the hour always seemed to end too soon. In the months that followed, as Linda exposed the truth about her childhood experiences, she became progressively more animated. During her second year of therapy, there was also a remarkable change in her physical appearance, and I realized that she was actually pretty. Her facial expression changed from a childish pout into a soft, feminine smile. She seemed to blossom into womanhood in a relatively short time frame; and with no deliberate effort, she shed twenty pounds. I remember thinking that, if nothing else, the sessions were helpful to her in relation to the once-persistent weight issue.

Linda's good looks were enhanced by her positive transference reaction, as well as by a feeling of genuine appreciation for her therapeutic progress. She exhibited a newfound belief in herself and started to feel her own strength. She began dating, an activity that she had had little experience with, and had avoided completely for the previous two years. I remember once, in the middle of the night, she called me through my answering service in a panic to tell me that she had been sexual with a man she had just met. She expected to be punished or condemned. Her shame gradually dissipated as we spoke. By the time she came in for her next session, she was more calm and objective about the situation.

Later, she met and fell in love with a man named Bill Janes. She introduced him to me, and they had a couple of joint sessions to smooth over the rough edges in their relationship. Basically, he was a good person, but at times he had a tendency to switch into becoming irritable and critical. I remember Linda referring to him as either Bill or "The Hulk," depending on which persona he was manifesting. This reference became a kind of ongoing joke among her friends, but eventually the situation worked itself out. Bill stayed himself most of the time and was sweet and affectionate. After Linda terminated therapy, they were married in the picturesque town of Nikko, Japan, and honeymooned throughout Asia.

Toward the end of her sessions, Linda wrote about her experiences during her therapy with me. Just before leaving for Japan, she presented this excerpt from her journal to me as a gift. In my practice, this was an unusual gesture, and I was touched emotionally.

> I still remember the first time I saw Dr. Firestone. I was sitting in the reception room of his office, nervous because I was about to involve myself in therapy for the third time. The first two attempts were practically inconsequential in terms of affecting the essence of me, though I thought I had really put my heart into those efforts.
>
> His waiting room was empty. It was small and sparsely furnished, but comfortable. I arrived early because I was worried about finding the right place and I didn't want to be late. I had about a half hour to wait for my session. During those thirty minutes, my anxiety and self-consciousness about the impending

meeting steadily increased. What would Dr. Firestone be like? How would I ever be able to talk to a complete stranger at all, much less reveal my innermost thoughts and feelings? Why was I here?

About five minutes to four, I flicked up the waiting-room switch to announce my presence. By this time, my heart was thumping so hard that I could feel it inside my chest. The last three minutes seemed endless. Finally, I heard the sound of the inner-office door open, and Dr. Firestone appeared. He was good-looking, about six feet tall, and I guessed his age to be late thirties or early forties. He introduced himself and showed me down the corridor into his office.

At the time, I couldn't begin to put my initial reaction into words, even in my own mind. I existed on two levels simultaneously. On the one hand, I was awkwardly attempting to attend to the practical matters at hand. I had to answer some preliminary questions about my background and my reasons for being there. But more importantly, on another level I was trying to assimilate the impact of meeting a person who, even at first glance, was different from any person I had met during my 21 years of life.

I was taken off guard by how open to me his face was, especially his eyes. They were alive and warm. He really looked at me. I felt both his presence and my own in a way I never had before. It terrified me and intrigued me, each to the extreme. In an instant I knew that if I proceeded wholeheartedly with this therapy, something would happen within me that would be qualitatively different from anything I had experienced before. At that same moment, I understood that my previous encounters with counseling had been filled with psychological jargon and platitudes. In the presence of this unusual human being, I sensed that there was room for honest disclosure.

What I realized in the flash of a second about Dr. Firestone proved to be true one hundred times over during the three years of my weekly therapy sessions. He was a human being in the fullest sense of the word. And it was precisely this humanness that allowed me to begin to find that same quality in myself. He did not pose as the expert, the doctor, different in kind from me. We were two equal people, sitting together in a room, trying to acknowledge truths that I had never before been permitted the freedom to utter.

I had always been an extremely shy, quiet person and had never spoken to anyone without censoring myself. Understandably, it took me a long time, actually many months, to come to trust Dr. Firestone enough to really talk with him. There were so many sessions where I came in wanting desperately to communicate a simple thought but found myself unable to do so. The fifty minutes would pass agonizingly slowly, with me barely able to eke out a word. On the one hand I knew I could trust him completely, but on the other I could not believe that a person like he appeared to be could actually exist. But once I started talking, I couldn't stop. I more than made up for my long years of silence. From then on my sessions were the most intriguing part of my life.

Six months before Linda terminated therapy, I had started my first psychotherapy group. Membership in the newly formed venture was carefully considered: I selected four men and four women who were in the process of terminating individual therapy. They were people who were well-developed and self-possessed. I admired them for their intelligence, their spirit of independence, their honesty, and their abiding interest in psychology. Linda was one of these eight people.

When the day of that first group meeting arrived, I was nervous and excited. I was moved by the fact that each of these people, whom I knew so well and had a deep affection for, would now be getting to know each other. I was eager to see how they would interact. I felt anxious and slightly sick to my stomach as I opened the door to let everyone in. But as they filed in looking cheerful, fresh, and very much alive, and I sat down at my desk, I had a profound feeling that this was where I belonged.

This group became the highlight of the week for all involved. As the months passed, the members grew closer and more trusting of one another. They spoke openly about their anger, sexuality, and competitive feelings, not intellectually or in the abstract, but directly in response to one another. These people were driving hard toward a better life. Regardless of their problems and personal handicaps, they were strongly committed to the openness and honesty that they shared for that hour and a half each week. The way in which this group of people valued their freedom and the democratic process inspired me. I felt better as a human being and as a therapist.

In her journal, Linda reflected back on her impressions of the group.

Dr. Firestone said that he had the idea of forming a therapy group with patients who were nearing the end of therapy. I had seen him once a week during my therapy session, which was 50 minutes a week and that was it. When he told me this idea, I was thrilled. I was glad for the chance to continue talking with him, because he was the only person I had ever honestly talked to.

I had developed quite a bit personally in the course of the therapy, but I was not a person who felt comfortable in groups at all. I hated groups. I was scared. I was uncomfortable, very unsure of myself. These were total strangers, except they weren't exactly strangers because I knew that each of them had gone through something in their own way that was like what I had gone through. And I was excited at the idea of being able to talk truthfully. I never had talked truthfully with anybody before my therapy, and here were people who maybe I could have a similar kind of dialogue with.

We decided that in this group it would be a first-name basis for all of us. So I started calling Dr. Firestone "Bob." Our talks were straightforward, extremely honest. They were direct and sometimes maybe a little bit harsh. I wouldn't say we weren't compassionate, but if we had to sacrifice either compassion or honesty, we would err in the direction of honesty, which we thought had its own value. Very, very honest about what was going on right at the moment, with competitive feelings and even sexual attractions to people, right there in the room.

After about a month or so, I still had said hardly anything in the group meetings; I had been mostly listening. Then Matt, who seemed to be a very angry guy, challenged Bob's leadership of the group. I remember him saying something like, "Why the hell are you in charge? This is supposed to be a democratic process. If that's so, why are you sitting behind that desk? I don't hear you talking about your problems. You should participate like everyone else." Then he actually said, "Fuck you, and your god-damned superiority!"

This assault took me by such surprise. It wasn't the content; I was used to hearing and saying all kinds of angry things. It was the ferocity of Matt's feelings that got to me. I immediately felt protective of Bob. Without even waiting to see if he was going to say anything for himself, I blew up at Matt. I remember yelling something like, "Bob's a regular guy who is respectful and not in any way superior. He's really open and honest about himself. It's ridiculous to say that he's hiding behind his desk." I felt great from getting mad at Matt, and there was definitely less tension in the room. Even Bob seemed relieved.

Then Bob suggested that Matt could lead the group if he liked. Matt agreed to the proposal and immediately offered a suggestion that we try a technique that he had read about in an article on sensitivity training. He told us to make a circle, hold hands and close our eyes; then after three minutes, open our eyes and share our feelings. Hardly any of us wanted to participate; it seemed contrived and gimmicky and cutesy. Someone even said it was stupid. At that point, Matt turned to Bob and whined, "They won't listen to me. It's not right. Can't you get them to participate?" We all started laughing at the irony of his remarks. At first Matt was confused, but then he caught on and joined in the laughter.

Sometime later, Bob told me that Matt's hostility had gotten to him, and that he had been sitting in the group with anger building inside him. He had been startled when I attacked Matt, especially because I had been so quiet up to then. He had also been touched by my sentiments and by my defense of him.

After we had been meeting for about a year, Brad, one of the original members of the group, brought up the issue of socializing together. He said that he really wanted to go out and have coffee with all of us afterwards. I was intrigued by the idea, I wanted to do it, and so did everybody else. We wondered what Bob would say and waited anxiously for his decision, but we kind of already knew that as group members we weren't supposed to meet outside of the office setting. When Bob responded, he emphasized that point because he felt that it was necessary in order to preserve the integrity of the group process.

We wanted to honor Bob's request because going out together really would be a deviation from what he had envisioned. Then Brad asked if he would throw us out if we went against his advice, and I remember Bob saying he couldn't bring himself to throw us out, but he continued warning that it wasn't a good idea.

But we went out anyway. This became the nicest part of my social life at the time. I loved it! Going to coffee after the group, we laughed and joked around a lot. With a person you might have expressed the strongest, most angry feeling toward in the group session, you were congenial and friendly toward afterwards. There was nobody I was closer to in my life than the people in that talk. They knew more about me and I knew more about them than I did about anybody.

Linda began to talk openly about herself in the group setting much as she had in her individual sessions with me. She came to care deeply for the other members, and she expressed her feelings in a straightforward way. Not only had Linda become an attractive woman, but everyone in the group was positively affected by her warmth and concern. Her perceptions and insights were clear and valuable to the others. She spoke with compassion about the struggles of each person. Moreover, her kindness and tolerance for feeling were contagious.

Reading her journal, I was struck by how much Linda had changed from the wretched, shy girl I had first met. I was pleased to remember her progress in therapy and the early indications of her potential strength. The Linda I came to know was very direct, honest, and outspoken. I was particularly moved by her coming to my defense in the group. Thinking of the irony of the situation makes me smile. This once practically mute person had stood up for me with a powerful verbal response.

Linda emerged as a mature, vital, and self-confident person—a lovely, vibrant woman with flashing eyes and a radiant smile. In addition to feeling good personally, she exhibited a great deal of appreciation for the therapeutic process and had a serious desire to enter the profession. After getting her bachelor's degree, she enrolled in a graduate program in clinical psychology and later became a practicing psychologist. She went on to make a meaningful contribution, offering her personal experience, self-knowledge, and compassion to help so many others.

CHAPTER 11

DADDY'S GIRL

first heard about Lori Anderson from David Klein, a client of mine who was a psychologist and happened to be her next-door neighbor. He described a pretty blond-haired, blue-eyed girl who was about eight years old at the time. She was his son's playmate and appeared to be an unusually intelligent, sweet youngster. Of course, many years had passed since that conversation, and by this time Lori was in her midthirties.

She was a typical California beauty with long hair and a spectacular figure, and she seemed to be quite self-possessed. When she sought my services, she had been divorced for several years, was working as a successful realtor, and owned her own company. She mentioned that there was a man in her life, Bernard, whom she loved and respected, but complained that the relationship was complicated and troublesome. She liked his warmth and affection, but at times she found herself disinterested and also irritable. At those times, Bernard would become angry and they would quarrel. She knew instinctively that there was something self-destructive in the way she related to men in general and to Bernard in particular.

After our preliminary discussion, I accepted Lori as a client and we agreed to meet for two sessions a week. My initial impression was that beneath her calm, unruffled exterior, she was fundamentally insecure. I also sensed that she was not being entirely frank with me. She acted like a person with some sort of secret. Nevertheless, she seemed congenial and I expected that our sessions would work out favorably.

In our first meeting, I asked her to tell me a little about her background. "Well, I don't really know where to start. Let's see. I was always told I was a 'good baby'—didn't cry or ask for much. My first memories are from around age three or four. One time I received a doll as a present and my older brother, Jeff, got a car that he could pedal around. I felt awful because I had asked for a car instead of the doll. That kind of tells a story. I never felt like they listened to me."

"I can see that you were disappointed. What was your family like?"

"I don't remember ever being held or comforted by my mom, unless there was some sort of tragedy, like when my horse was killed when I was fifteen. She stayed by my bed for two days; I couldn't stop crying. I do remember her and my sister, Patty, always hanging on each other. Even though consciously I didn't feel jealous—I was cruel to Patty for as far back as I can remember—it was impossible for me not to pinch her, hit her, and humiliate her.

"After I saw the *Wizard of Oz* when I was five or six, I had a recurring nightmare of the Wicked Witch. Obviously the witch was my mother. Those words, 'I'll get you, my pretty!' stuck deep in my subconscious. It seemed like that's what she secretly felt toward me. I can't imagine not telling my own daughter that she looks pretty—I never remember my mother saying that to me, ever.

"My brother and I became very close when I was around nine or ten. Before that, he used to beat up Patty and me all the time. Jeff and I were so inseparable that my father became very suspicious and jealous. He set rules so that we couldn't be alone in the same room with the door closed. This seemed so weird, but it exemplified his hatred of Jeff and his possessiveness of me."

"That seems pretty significant."

"I know. One of the worst traumas I remember was one night when we were all having dinner together. I was probably six or seven. Jeff was playing around, and my mom and sister and I were laughing. My father was glaring at Jeff. I guess it was because he seemed to be getting all the attention. I could see that something terrible was about to happen, and I felt scared. My father was becoming more and more agitated. Finally, he exploded at Jeff and hit the table with his fist. The pounding caused a piece of hot meatloaf to fly into Patty's eye. All hell broke loose. Patty had to be rushed off to the emergency room and my father screamed at Jeff, 'That's it—pack your bags—I'm dropping you off in the middle of nowhere and you are out of here for good!'

"I went catatonic. I couldn't move or speak. My mother snapped at me, 'What is it? What's wrong with you?' I couldn't even move my mouth. Patty was crying and Jeff was sobbing in a corner. This scene still breaks my heart today. It terrified me to think that someone would throw a child out into the world by himself.

"At the last minute, my father retracted his threat, but for some absurd reason, this event intensified my hatred toward Patty. I thought that her being babied had led to Jeff's being abused and also to me being rejected."

"It appears you had a pretty rough family situation. Your father seems like he was not only possessive and jealous but also somewhat out of control and violent. And you describe your mother as cold and aloof. Besides that, you hated your sister, and things with your brother were, at the least, complicated. We'll have to go more deeply into all of these matters and come to understand how they affected you. But let's talk some more about the reasons that brought you here."

"I've been feeling sort of down, but it's more like my life feels screwed up. My work is good, but my relationships are a different story. I keep messing up. I told you that I like this guy, Bernard, but lately things are getting worse. We are basically really good together. I know that I love him and he loves me, so it's stupid for us to fight. I know it's my fault. It seems like every time it's going great, I freak out. I just pull away.

"I began to notice that right after we've been really close, I'll start picking him apart in my mind. Like I tell myself he's gotten kind of dull, he's not as attractive as he used to be, and making love doesn't seem as exciting. Sometimes I'll feel down on myself, like I'm not as great as he thinks I am. He's just being nice to me, like he's stupid to love me. Mean things like that. I'll act irritable or start a fight, then things aren't so great."

I recognized that Lori was describing her critical inner voices toward Bernard and toward herself, but I decided not to pursue the subject in her first session. She probably would have been open to it; however, I intuitively sensed that she was hiding something more important that needed to be addressed.

"You're saying that it's a pattern for you to ruin things with him when they are going well. I wonder what goes into that." Lori ignored my prompt, and her thoughts took a new direction. She seemed nervous.

"Things were going perfect for the longest time and we even talked about getting married. But there's another thing," She looked sheepish and admitted that she felt embarrassed about what she was about to say.

"When I was in Taiwan for a job on one of my trips for work, I met another man. George was the project manager for the hotel I was trying to broker. Well, we, uh, uh . . . went out for drinks, and . . . I felt very sexually attracted to him. You know, then later that night we got involved. Well, since then, I can't get him out of my mind. We've been getting together like this for a while. We talk all the time, and he plans to visit the States. He really likes me, too. But I have a funny feeling, like I'm fucking up my whole life and I don't know what to do. So that's my story."

"I can appreciate your dilemma, and I know that you are confused."

"But what should I do?" Lori exclaimed. "You're supposed to help!"

I could tell that she was beginning to feel angry because my comment suggested my reluctance to offer direction or advice. I responded by telling her that it was critical that she develop a full understanding of her motives before making any important decisions in her life. I concluded the session by saying, "You were smart to seek help at this time. I really believe that you can get someplace with these issues. We have to stop for right now, but I can see you next Monday."

When Lori left my office, I thought about her current situation and wondered about her relationships with men. Even though I had learned a little about her family, I wanted to know more about how it was affecting her present state of mind.

In relation to her distancing behavior with Bernard, I was reminded of an article that I had written about why people often respond negatively to being loved or especially acknowledged.[1] My basic thesis was that being exceptionally valued leads to an identity crisis when it conflicts with a person's character as it was defined within the family. When there is emotional pain and rejection in childhood, people form a negative self-image and build defenses in an attempt to avoid being hurt again. A deep love relationship causes them to feel particularly vulnerable, and often there is a recurrence of painful emotions from the past. Second, in the new situation, they may feel a deep sadness or become increasingly anxious; generally they suffer some sense of disequilibrium. Last, being close to another person in a loving relationship makes them aware that life is precious but must eventually be surrendered. If we embrace life and love, we must also face the inevitability of death.

Usually these responses are not part of people's conscious awareness, and they react by finding fault with or creating distance between themselves and the person who loves them. I wondered if Lori was indirectly suggesting in her session that the reason she sought this new relationship was an attempt to destroy the intimacy with Bernard and restore her psychological equilibrium. I knew that my hypothesis would be tested in the sessions that followed.

In our next meeting, Lori expanded her account of growing up in what appeared to me to be a largely dysfunctional family. I was primarily concerned about her father's abnormal fixation on her.

"I remember my father staring at me after I reached puberty, like in a sexual way. All of a sudden he began watching me like a hawk—where I was, the boys I was with, what I was wearing. One day when I was thirteen, he made me change my clothes into a 'less slutty' look before I left for a party. I was furious and embarrassed by his trying to control my every move. He went on from being suspicious of Jeff to include all the other guys I knew.

"His crazy focus peaked on a family trip to Hawaii. I was out in the ocean on a surfboard. I was paddling around when I saw him jumping up and down on shore, waving to me wildly. I got so scared. I thought a shark was behind me! When I got closer, I recognized his all-too-familiar red, bloated, angry face. I could hear him yelling, 'Your boobs are hanging out of your swimsuit! You look disgraceful. Get out of the water right now!' I felt so ashamed and embarrassed. I knew then that he was totally nuts."

"You must have felt pretty bad."

"I really did. Later, when I was in college, I mentioned to him that I was switching my major in school from math to art. I had been doing well in math, but I wanted to pursue what I was really interested in. His face turned bright red and he screamed, 'What the hell do you want? Do you want to become a prostitute?' I was shocked and furious, and humiliated, too. The whole family was out to eat in a restaurant and people in the nearby booths could clearly hear him.

"My father always acted like I belonged to him, like I was not only his possession, but like he actually wanted me to be like him. Could he even have wanted to be me?"

"It's possible. That's sometimes the case with men who have such an intense focus on their daughters."

"He hated Jeff so violently and was so obsessed with me that Patty didn't really exist to him. His focus makes me think that maybe he hated himself and his maleness so much that he actually wished he was a pretty girl. He projected all his self-hatred as a man onto Jeff and could barely contain himself from actually killing him.

"I watched helplessly as Jeff turned the hatred that was directed at him into his own self-loathing. He lost his confidence as a male and probably wished he was a girl, too. It was safer for him just as it must have been for my father, whose own father had hated him a generation before. My grandfather was supposed to have been a real bastard, too. The whole sexual role-reversal thing in my family is crazy."

"I'm impressed by your insight. You seem to have an unusual psychological understanding." I genuinely admired Lori's perceptiveness about the dynamics of her family. She was obviously an intuitive person psychologically.

Lori's therapy progressed. She spoke of growing up in the hills behind Santa Cruz, California, a scenic locale marked by beautiful natural surroundings of mountains and ocean. When she initially mentioned the idyllic community, I felt envious and wished that my own children could be growing up in such a wholesome environment. I was truly surprised and disappointed to find out otherwise. Life for children raised around Santa Cruz during Lori's teenage years was, in fact, a living hell.

"I started to sneak out in the middle of the night with friends to get stoned, partly to rebel against my father's overpowering focus on me. It was always exhilarating and fun to outsmart our parents. By the time I was fifteen, all levels of drugs were available to us, so the escape and secrecy were mandatory. It was fun a period of time until tragedy started to strike. Two boys I was close to shot themselves to death, one on his sixteenth birthday, leaving a note saying 'Happy Birthday, everyone'; the other had just suffered a breakup with his girlfriend.

"Then the worst nightmare of all was when my best friend's eighteen-year-old brother shot their twelve-year-old sister in the head with a single bullet. He'd had a terrible reaction to LSD. He was having a bad trip while he was at home alone with her. A 'voice' told him to save her from the misery of this life. The entire community was devastated; there were so many drug overdoses, too many to recount. I left it all behind at the age of nineteen; I never reconnected with my old friends because the memories were too painful. Even driving up the coast toward Santa Cruz these days shakes me up. It was a tragic, terrible time. What a sad loss of young lives; I'm grateful to have survived."

Lori was anxious to discuss her sexual history. She said that most of her friends had been accustomed to nudity and had spent a lot of time hiking and camping naked. She told me that on one occasion, she had been arrested for lying on the beach completely "au naturel."

She continued, "Here's what I know about my sexuality. I remember liking boys from a young age, and my best friends on my street were two guys. We hunted for snakes and lizards, and found secret hiding places to play in. I loved being outdoors and creating my own world, away from the dark, depressing, unhappy house where my mother was asleep all day and my brother was glued to the TV.

"Jeff and I were pretty close when we were kids, sort of desperate and emotionally dependent on each other. He told me that we explored each other sexually, even though I don't actually remember anything about this myself. He said that when we were as old as eleven or twelve, we would watch television and casually touch each other sexually. It's odd that I have no memory of these things, given how old I was."

"You must have felt pretty uncomfortable or ashamed."

"I guess so. For one thing, my father would have gone crazy if he had known.

"Later, there was this one man at junior college who was a teacher of mine. I'd known him for a few months. I thought it was just a natural feeling, sort of a friendship. I started to go out with him right before my parents went to Europe one year. Up until the day before I left for summer vacation, it hadn't been sexual; and then we were. At the time, I didn't think that there was anything strange about it.

"Looking back at my choice of men, I notice that I was either drawn toward safe, boyish men (my first boyfriend was actually named Jeff, like my brother) who were more like siblings—compatible, fun, not successful, non-threatening. Or else men who were vain, sort of feminine, superior—like my father and the teacher I was drawn to. Both types were easy to manipulate.

"My ex-husband, James, was more the first type. He was slightly younger than me—I was twenty-one at the time. He was very charming in his pursuit of me, and I was flattered by his attention and interest. Later we got married, and suddenly we were bound to each other. It wasn't a good choice for me. I was ambivalent about ever getting tied by law to anyone. It made me resentful. I felt angry at him; it seemed like he expected too much. For five years, we were still kind of loving to each other, but at times he was insecure and I was often distant. There was some difficulty in our sexual relationship after we had our two boys. I felt myself more interested in them than in him. Toward the end, we started arguing and fighting. He became even more jealous and insecure, and that made it worse. After ten years, we got divorced.

"The first man in my life who didn't fit either type was Bernard. I really fell in love with him. He is strong, very masculine, not vain, and he loves women. He is free, adventurous, smart, and expects me to be strong, too—not to be a little girl. This has been the biggest struggle in our relationship. When I behave like an adult woman, he's really drawn to me. My tolerance for this is the main issue in my life today. It has always felt safe for me to be childish, self-hating, afraid of other women, too controlling. These were traits I learned early on in order to survive."

"I agree that these are the key issues for you. It seems that you felt guilty about competing with your mother because she remained in the background. You mentioned that she was depressed, let herself go, and shied away from being feminine. For you to embrace your femininity and sexuality was to break the connection with her. That was frightening and left you feeling very much alone."

"You know, I never thought about it like that. I guess that's why I'm afraid of other women, too. I expect them to want to get back at me."

"If you deny your own anger and competitive feelings, you project them onto other women and fear retaliation. When that fear is aroused, you tend to back away from competing and remain childish in order to feel safe. By the way, this is an important factor in your relationship with men. It explains some of your anxiety and intolerance of closeness."

In the months that followed, Lori progressed quickly and I enjoyed working with her. She was determined to understand herself and how she interacted with others. She began to untangle the relationship with George.

"When I met George in Taiwan, I had been feeling closer to Bernard and we were talking seriously about having a baby together. Something I had wanted for a long time. This alone may have sent me running to the other side of the world."

"That makes a good deal of sense. Do you remember what you were thinking or feeling at the time?"

"I know I started to feel critical of Bernard, just like I used to feel after we'd been really close. I was also very anxious. But what was making me so nervous at this point was the thought of having a baby with Bernard, just trying to picture myself as a mother. I had never even considered having kids, maybe because of the way I felt as a child."

"What did you think when you pictured yourself as a mother?"

"Just that Bernard was crazy to want to have a baby with me, that a kid would tie us down, that I wouldn't know what to do with a baby. I know this sounds weird, and I wasn't thinking like this all of the time, but when I *did* have these thoughts, I would get really anxious, a panicky feeling almost. Sometimes it was hard to shut off the thoughts and images."

"Try to say more about those thoughts."

"How do you mean? That's about all there was."

"Just say more of your thoughts about being a mother, but try to say them like someone is telling you that's what's going to happen. Like a prediction . . . 'You won't know what to do with a baby,' and so on . . . "

"Oh, I think I get it. *'Look, you're crazy to even think about having a baby. You won't know what to do. What if you drop it, or something even worse? What are you thinking? Are you crazy? You can't have an independent life with a kid! You'll never get away or be able to travel like you do now. You're so stupid! Don't say I didn't warn you . . . '"*

The process of expressing her thoughts as though someone else were saying them to her, or *against* her, brought out strong feelings, and Lori began to cry softly.

"God, I had no idea I was thinking those things. It's like my mother's voice telling me I shouldn't have a baby. She always told us to be quiet in the house, said we were driving her crazy. I can see why I was so ambivalent about getting pregnant. I think I was really confused, trying to come to a decision when I first met George. I was scared, too."

"What you said is important. I think you're on the right track."

"Yeah. I can see now what was going on in my head when I went to Taiwan.

"Objectively, I couldn't understand my strong physical attraction to George in the first place. When I first met him, I was giving a presentation in front of twenty-five people and I barely even noticed him. Still, he was well-groomed and had a charming British accent. He seemed so interested in everything he could find out about me. Then romantic feelings started to come over me. I returned home feeling very confused and guilty but also couldn't stop thinking about him. He wrote me some very passionate letters that left me even more interested.

"When I returned to Asia a few weeks later, the attraction toward him had only increased, so I gave into the feelings and began an intense affair that lasted for months. Finally, I decided I would have to tell Bernard everything because he probably knew anyway. I was traveling with two of my associates whom Bernard knew, and they were aware of my obvious flirtation."

"How did Bernard react when you told him?"

"When I talked about everything openly, he felt pretty bad, but he wasn't punishing. After many long, painful conversations, we decided to still try to work on our relationship, but I told him that I wasn't quite ready to give up George. Bernard was not too pleased about that. Since then, there have been lots of ups and downs and I don't know what to do."

"You're feeling confused," I reflected.

"From some of the other things I've been talking about with you, I've started to see that George has many characteristics similar to my father. There's a déjà vu feeling of both sexual attraction and repulsion that has started to evolve in that relationship. It's beginning to bother me a lot. Why would I go for a man like my father, whom I despised?"

"That's an interesting question. What do you think about it?"

"I don't get it. Maybe I was trying to work something out with him from the past, some leftover ambivalence."

"That makes a lot of sense. I hope that you benefit from identifying your self-attacks about having a baby with Bernard, and also the insights you had concerning the ambivalent feelings you were experiencing right before you met George. Your mixed feelings toward your father may also explain part of your attraction to George. You are both drawn to and repelled by your father, but you must not deny the first part, the pull toward him. That relationship, as complex as it was, has had a huge negative impact on your life. Understanding it can help you feel better."

In the sessions that followed, we talked a good deal more about Lori's ambivalent feelings toward her father, her attraction to him and her feelings of revulsion and hatred. Facing these emotions and developing more understanding of the sources and implications of her negative thinking eventually helped her to feel calm. After a few weeks, she sized up her situation.

"To tell you the truth, I'm beginning to think seriously about ending things with George. Finally, after going back and forth for a while, I think I'm starting to get my head straight about this. It's sort of a logical decision. I'm sure that Bernard is going to feel good about this, too."

After Lori broke up with George, her life began to stabilize on all fronts. Her relationship with Bernard was flourishing and her business was going well. I respected how she processed insights and utilized them for her emotional growth and development. In her case, changing her perceptions of past events usually led to immediate positive actions. Lori was in excellent spirits, and we began talking about termination.

Then, late one night, she was notified that her father had died of a heart attack. She had known that he had been suffering from a terminal illness with only a short time to live, but the news was still shocking. Lori told me that in his last years, her father had begun therapy and stopped drinking. He had become a softer person and had actually been a kind grandfather to her children. His drastic personality change was surprising to her, yet she continued to maintain a cordial, yet distant, relationship with him. In the sessions that followed, she spoke about her reaction to his death.

"When I was called the night he died, I slammed the phone down and all I wanted to do was to go back to sleep. I was angry at the call and didn't feel like dealing with the harsh reality. My brother and sister were both devastated, and I felt angry at their hypocrisy. Here was a man who had ruined our lives, and they were acting like they couldn't handle his passing. What bullshit! I could understand his close friends and peers mourning his loss; but on a deep level, I knew I could never forgive him for how he terrorized our entire childhoods. He was like Hitler and we were his Jews.

"His funeral was last week, and I arranged to be out of town during it because I couldn't bear to feel my angry, complicated feelings. On that trip, I noticed I was drinking more than my usual glass or two of wine. Social drinking has always been easy for me, and I have always felt in control of it at any party or gathering. Last week the hotel minibar suddenly seemed very appealing because I could drink alone and as much as I wanted. This seemed to help me 'de-stress' and fall into a badly needed sleep.

"It's obvious to me that I've had a weird reaction to his dying, but I can't tell what's what. One thing that I know is that I was cut off from my emotions about the event when I heard about it, and ever since, too."

I told Lori that I felt concerned about her reaction and offered to help her deal with any sadness that came up. I was worried about her suffering any adverse effects from her father's death.

In my experience, there are many potentially negative psychological reactions to the death of a parent or caretaker. However, there are two reactions that are particularly detrimental to the survivors. One, they tend to take on or reinforce critical negative thoughts and attitudes toward themselves representative of their past association with the deceased. And two, they tend to incorporate undesirable character traits of the parent into their own personalities and behavior. Both are an attempt to symbolically reconnect to the person, deny the loss, and reduce death anxiety. Oddly enough, these reactions are usually more pronounced in people when the person who died has had a destructive influence on them. Unfortunately, both of these themes played a significant part in Lori's feelings and behavior following her father's death.

What started out as a minor binge after her father's death became a more serious problem for Lori over the next couple of years. Her drinking was a major topic of our sessions for that time period. "Some people are concerned about me. Bernard has mentioned it to me a number of times. And so have some of my friends. They think that I have a drinking problem, but I don't think they're right. Since they seemed so concerned, I told them I would stop drinking except for socially."

Later, she spoke about several occasions when she couldn't remember how much she had had to drink, and she had woken up disoriented and ashamed.

"It seems like Bernard and your friends are right. You've been deceiving yourself and them all the while, but you know what you've been doing. I want you to accept that you have become an alcoholic. If you don't face it, there is no chance for positive change."

"I don't think it's that dramatic. I still think that I can handle my drinking. I promise that I will stop drinking to excess. I feel like it would be giving up on myself if I say that I can't handle liquor. I'm stronger than that. I know that I have the willpower."

What followed were months of denial and outright lying to me, and I began to feel alienated from her. Lori convinced me that she was not only *not* drinking, but had also given up smoking. When she later admitted that she had been lying to me about both, I felt foolish for having believed her. I always tend to trust my clients, so it feels really bad to be lied to. It's not that I'm naive but that I find it to be illogical that clients would deceive me; it just isn't in their interest. Of course, people lie even to themselves, so why should I be surprised? I was determined to work through any negative counter-transference reactions I was having toward Lori and to help her get back on track.

Eventually, even her business started to suffer, and for some reason that gave her the motivation to begin to tackle the problem in earnest. Gradually, she achieved insight into the entire process.

"Since my father's death, work has become more and more stressful for me. I have become convinced that I need to travel more and work harder in order to keep my company going. I realize that I have incorporated my father's intense desire for me to succeed into my inner psyche. I'm killing myself to be the 'good girl' who works so hard to please him. Instead of mourning him or really saying good-bye, I've morphed his driving and unforgiving traits into myself.

"I'm always under pressure at work, but I think a lot of the pressure is coming from me. I keep telling myself things like, '*Look, this presentation has to be really good! And stop putting it off, stop procrastinating! You know you have to finish the estimates tonight! Everybody is depending on you to deliver it tomorrow. You can't let them down. Look, just pull it together and do it! And it damn well better be good!'*

"I've even alienated people who have always loved working for me. I'm so critical; their presentations have to be absolutely perfect and there's no room for any mistakes. My nightmares are filled with angry clients who need to be placated or else I will be killed. I feel like I am back in my family, trying to keep the peace at all costs so no one will get murdered. But, during all of this, I can see that I've become more and more like him. I feel bad but I can't seem to get out of this downward spiral."

"You can get out of it, but you must understand how the loss of your father caused you to identify more strongly with him—not just the drinking part, but also his mean attitude toward people and his pressure to succeed. Besides that, the voice attacks you just expressed indicate that you've turned on yourself and begun to feel miserable. That's your way of holding on to him."

"I think I'm starting to understand." Lori paused, "And my pessimistic attitude is just part of the whole thing. The more pessimistic and depressed I feel, the more I think about having a drink.

"One of the ways I psych myself up to get through an 'all-nighter' whenever I feel pressured to finish a project is to tell myself that I can always relax once it's over, or the next evening, with a drink. I think things like, *'You really aced that presentation, now you can have a drink. You can go back to your room and veg out, raid the minibar, watch TV. You deserve it after all the hard work you put in.'*

"Then I lose track of everything, including what I'm drinking and how much I drink. Then the next morning I can't remember much of what went on after a certain point. Did my associate drop over or not, did we have drinks together, or what? It's scary that I can't remember the details."

"I'm glad that you're scared. But I'm certain that you can get better and feel good again. You've got to accept the fact that you don't just have a 'drinking problem.' You are clearly an alcoholic and it's about time that you admit it to yourself. First, you've got to stop drinking altogether and then you have to discover more about the underlying causes that led up to your addiction."

"I know that you're right. I've begun to drink secretly and strategically. I wasn't going to tell you this. I'm so embarrassed. But a few weeks ago, I went to an event in New York and drank a lot of wine and then stopped for more drinks at a bar afterward. I was so drunk that I tripped and fell in the street. My face was bleeding and some strangers helped me back to my hotel. I had made previous plans to meet up with some family and friends who were traveling in New York too, and luckily they were in the lobby when I stumbled in. They were so helpful, I was so upset and they helped me to cope with my horrible destructive thoughts, and compassionately they put me to bed. As soon as I woke up in the morning, I was horrified at the incident. When I saw how badly I'd smashed my face on the sidewalk, I realized that I actually could have died. I was mortified when I thought of telling Bernard. But when I called him, he broke my heart. He was so compassionate and loving. All he wanted was for me to take care of myself and get help.

"One of the things that I felt the worst about was that the next day my fifteen-year-old nephew, Dan, gave me an earful. I helped raise him, and he is very dear to me. His anger and disappointment hit me deeply. He said that he was through with me; I had lied to him and he said he could never trust me again. I think what really hit me the hardest was that here was someone who had loved me so much his whole life, and I had shattered his innocent belief in me. This made me more determined than ever to stop drinking."

"I think you need additional help, and I suggest that the best way to deal with your alcoholism is to join Alcoholics Anonymous. Their first objective is that the person must admit up front that he or she is an addict. Besides, sharing your story with others who are fighting similar battles is the most effective way to deal with it. AA has the best track record for long-term success."

"I have to admit this scares me, but I think I have to do it. It's time." She looked sad for a moment, then took a deep breath, "I'm going to take your advice. I'm going to call a business friend of mine who I know is in AA. A while ago, she suggested to me that I might have a problem when she noticed me drinking by myself at a hotel bar. She said, 'Don't think, just go to some AA meetings and see what happens.' I have never liked the thought of AA, but now I'm so scared about where I'm heading. I'll definitely do it."

Lori spent many months going to AA. Her job took her all over the country, so she attended meetings in Pittsburgh, New York, Los Angeles, Santa Barbara, wherever she happened to be at the time. As part of their twelve-step program, she confessed all of her lies and secrets to her friends and to me about the drinking that had gone on since her father's death. It was a difficult struggle for her to continue to reveal the destructive voices that had fueled her drinking, but this helped her to gain control over her impulse to drink whenever she was under pressure. And it was not without considerable pain that she expressed her self-attacks, remnants of her father's controlling tactics and his envy, resentment, and anger toward her for being a woman. There were a few setbacks, but she prevailed. She proved to herself that she could live without alcohol for an indefinite time, and her prospects in this regard are promising. Once again, I admired her determination and strength of character.

In her last session, she spoke of her progress. I was deeply touched by her words.

"I have stopped working like a maniac and have started to enjoy my life again. I've been sober and relaxed for a year and a half. My sexuality has returned as a priority for me over my drinking. My friendships are important to me; but most of all, I realize I don't need to live out my father's road map for my life. It's mine to do whatever I want with. I'm not bound to him or anyone else in my original family. I care about them, but I am a free agent.

"The years I spent drinking passed much too quickly. They were lost in an alcoholic haze. Now, I savor every precious moment with those I love, especially with Bernard. And my nephew and I are becoming friends again, and that means a lot to me."

R. D. LAING AND THE DIVIDED SELF

t was the summer of 1989, and my friends and I were vacationing in Europe. We had just crossed the Atlantic Ocean on our seventy-five-foot motor-sailor, *Tamara*, via Bermuda and the Azores Islands. The sail was exhilarating, and we made our first landfall in Gibraltar. From there, we cruised slowly along the south of Spain; visited the Spanish islands of Ibiza, Minorca, and Mallorca; encountered a storm in the Golfo de León; and eventually landed in Monaco.

After a few days spent enjoying the gambling, swimming, hiking, and outdoor movie theater in this beautiful city, we rented a couple of vans and left the port for a land trip. We were anxious to explore the surrounding countryside. Our first destination was to be Villa d'Este, Italy, on Lake Como where we planned to spend a few days. At noon, we stopped at the Riva boat factory at Sarnico on Lago d'Iseo for a look at their new fifty-foot powerboat. After the tour, the guide told us that the craft would be launched one week later. We couldn't resist the opportunity for a demo ride on that new boat, so we rearranged our itinerary to arrive back at the factory in time for the launching, which meant we would *end*, rather than start, the trip on Lake Como. That's when everything changed.

We canceled our reservations at Villa d'Este and made Innsbruck, Austria, our new destination. But when we arrived there, it was pouring rain. In the grey afternoon light, I pictured staying in the dismal city and rejected the idea. I suggested that we continue driving out into the scenic Austrian countryside in the hopes that the weather would clear up. I had a particular spot in mind, a lovely gasthaus where I had once stayed. I was anxious to show it to my second wife, Tam; she had never been there, and I knew she would love the cozy atmosphere. We managed to find the place, got rooms for the night, and had just finished a hearty meal when Joyce Catlett, my close friend and co-author, ran up to the table looking excited.

She said, "You're not going to believe this, but R. D. Laing lives about a mile from here!" At first, I didn't know what she was talking about. Then she explained that she had been placing an international phone call and the operator had asked what city she was calling from. When the woman at the front desk told her Going, Austria, Joyce recognized the name from a letter she had sent Laing. Immediately, she got his phone number from her office and asked if I wanted to call him. "Can you believe it?" she added, "You always wanted to meet him; well, here's your chance!"

Ronnie Laing was a psychiatrist who became famous in the sixties for his unconventional views about family life and society. He became a hero to the counterculture and was admired for his poetry, which he referred to as "knots." In the field, he was well-respected yet controversial, and even demonized by some. There were all kinds of contradictory stories swirling around about him. They depicted him as either a really brilliant, compassionate psychiatrist or some kind of raving, drunken lunatic.

As distant colleagues, we were familiar with each other's work and had admired one another for years, but we had never met. We had corresponded and exchanged a few long telephone calls, and Ronnie had written a foreword to my 1985 book, *The Fantasy Bond*. We had even extended invitations to each other from various locations around the world, but our schedules had never coincided.

When she heard the news from Joyce, Tam was so thrilled that she could barely contain her enthusiasm. She considered it an act of fate. For her, it was a dream come true. Ever since she had visited Ronnie with Joyce in London several years before, she believed that something very special would happen if he and I ever got together. She could not get over the amazing concatenation of events that had brought us together.

I was not so much surprised as concerned. The reason for my worry pertained to troublesome aspects of Laing's mixed reputation, which were verified by certain circumstances that had occurred during Tam's previous visit with him.

I had arranged to meet with Laing myself in London and was going to show him one of our documentary films detailing a therapy technique I had developed called voice therapy. Joyce had made the necessary arrangements, but at the last minute I wasn't available due to a scheduling problem. Joyce and I decided that she should go in my place, and Tam said that she wanted to go along. Then, since my friend and former professor, Stuart Boyd, was also interested in meeting Laing, we set it up for him and his wife, Nan, to join the group. Because both men were Scottish and close in age, and as they had both attended Edinburgh University and studied psychology, and since each was remarkably intelligent and witty, Tam and I thought that they would have a lot in common.

When the different parties arrived in London, they didn't know what to expect, but they were eager to see what would unfold. Tam tells the story of that first meeting:

> We met Laing in the afternoon at the home of one of his colleagues. Early on, the man informed us, "If Ronnie likes you, you will be invited to join him for dinner. But if he doesn't, you won't." We said, "Okay, that's fine." Then we were introduced to Ronnie, who was very warm and congenial.
>
> When we began showing the documentary, Ronnie said, "Wait, stop the film," and he went out of the room and came back with his daughter, Natasha, because he wanted her to see it. As he watched the film, it was obvious that he was engaged and was having a positive reaction. Afterward, Laing told me that he liked the way Bob was in it, that he could see that Bob was attuned to people and that he was a sensitive therapist. When we were

about to leave, he invited us to come back in the evening and join him for dinner.

That entire afternoon, Ronnie had been nothing but gracious. It was just a very nice, civilized meeting. So, we went back to our hotel and a few hours later we took a cab over to his home. We were knocking on the door for the longest time, but there was no answer. Finally, we heard somebody coming down the stairs.

Then Ronnie opens the door and we are confronted by a completely different personality. He is so drunk and sort of swaying, and he says, "Come on in." So we follow him up a flight of stairs and walk into the living room. His associate is there along with Ronnie's partner, Marguerite, and Stuart and Nan, who arrived before us. Everybody is sitting around awkwardly and Ronnie offers us a drink. We take a seat and start talking, but he doesn't sit down. He just keeps pacing around the room, pacing and more pacing.

At this point his associate, who's sitting on a white sofa, tries to make conversation by saying to me, "So tell me about Bob's ideas about the fantasy bond." Just then, Ronnie comes to a stop behind the guy and he starts to pour his glass of red wine on the guy's head and onto his white shirt. Marguerite panics and says in a high-pitched voice, "Ronnie, Ronnie, not *red* wine! It stains!" It was obvious that she could see where the evening was headed, and she was trying to interfere before everything went completely wrong.

And so then, Ronnie continues to wander around the room, and when he comes up to Stuart he says, "You have very nice shoes." And Stuart says, "Thank you. I got them in Scotland." Then he goes on, "And, you have very nice shoes, too. A fine, Scottish brogue," trying to make the Scottish connection. And Ronnie responds, "Thank you. I got them in Phoenix."

It was such a strange situation, but it was really funny, too. Ronnie is still wandering around the room, people are sort of socializing and chatting, but I can see that Marguerite is getting more and more anxious. When he says, "Let's open another bottle of champagne," she interrupts him, still with that high, nervous voice, "No, no, Ronnie. Let's go to the restaurant now."

So then we're walking toward the restaurant, which is just around the block from their house, and Stuart is in an agitated state so I say, "Stuart, don't worry. Nothing is going to happen. He's not going to hit you or anything like that." Stuart says, "That's not what I'm worried about. I'm worried that I'm going to hit *him*." And I reassure him, "Oh, I wouldn't worry about that."

When we arrive at the restaurant, we are seated at the table, with Marguerite and Ronnie's associate, but Ronnie still won't sit down. He's walking slowly and deliberately around the table. When the restaurant owner's little girl comes up to the table, Ronnie leans down and says, "Oh, hello, little girl. Let me tell you a joke." And Marguerite shrieks, "No, no, Ronnie! Don't tell her *that* joke!" So he goes back to circling.

He is just so irreverent. Then everyone is chatting and he suddenly says to Stuart, "Stuart, what kind of name is that?" When Stuart answers, he goes into a lengthy explanation about the derivation of his name. Ronnie appears to be listening to him and then he announces, "This Stuart is a cunt!" Stuart doesn't say anything, but I can see that Ronnie is getting to him.

When Marguerite asks him what he would like to order, he says, "I'm not going to order anything. I'm just going to drink." Finally, he sits down at the table and people are telling jokes. So, Nan tells a joke and Ronnie leans across the table and he says, "That is a stupid joke; that is a stupid, Los Angeles joke!" In desperation, Marguerite interjects, "Oh, no, Ronnie, she's from Scotland!" At this point, Stuart pushes his chair back from the table and shouts, "OK. I've had enough!" and as he stands up, he says, "Let's take this outside."

And he leaves, and Ronnie says to Marguerite, "Give me a couple of pounds. I'll buy him a drink in the pub next door." Ronnie leaves the restaurant, and Stuart's waiting outside on the sidewalk. He picks Ronnie up and throws him over a parked car and into the street. Ronnie gets to his feet, and these two older men actually start fighting. Their fistfight moves into the restaurant, and it's like a scene from a Western movie: they're fighting and hitting each other, tables are being knocked over, and plates are crashing and guests are scattering.

Finally, Marguerite drags Ronnie away and Stuart comes running over to Joyce and me and says, "You've got to get out of here. You're not safe." And I say, "Stuart, he has no issue with us. Why don't you and Nan leave and Joyce and I can stay here." So now it's just the two of us, and the associate, sitting at the table and we're talking. I say, "This is so strange." And he says, "Oh, no, this happens often." "Really?" I asked. "Yes. What he does is he'll pick out the dominant male figure in the setting and he'll goad him. It almost always leads to an argument or an actual fight and he ends up getting hit."

Soon Marguerite and Ronnie come back, and he's changed his shirt because he was bleeding from the fight, and his hand is bandaged up. So he sits down and he turns to me and says, "Where is he?" And I answer, "Where's who?" And he demands, "Where is Stuart?" And I say, "He left." And he says, "Call him!" And I counter, "No, *you* call him." Now he pushes his chair back and, holding his hand in the air, he declares, "Nobody does this to me and runs off!!" And I'm thinking, "Oh my God, these people are so immature." Marguerite, who is clearly at her wit's end, says, "Maybe we should go home now." To which I say, "Good idea. Let's just call it an evening." And so that was the end of our first meeting with Laing.

You can imagine how I felt, hearing this impossible story when Tam returned. I knew that everyone had a dark side, but this was beyond belief. Talk about the divided self!

Now the twice-changed agenda that day had uncannily brought Laing and me together in the same place. Joyce phoned him at his residence and found that he had arrived from Germany the night before and would be leaving for London the next morning. The long-awaited visit had to be arranged for that very evening; before we had time to digest our meal, Joyce, Tam, and I, along with two of our children—Lena, who was four at the time, and Ronnie, who was two—were on our way. Driving to his house, I kept saying over and over, like a mantra, "I'm not going to hit him no matter what happens. I'm not going to hit him."

Ronnie Laing was with a client when we arrived, so we visited with Marguerite in the living room. When he joined us, he was agitated and ill at ease. He once again remained standing; he paced the floor and then walked out onto the balcony; after a while, he returned to the room and paced some more. Then he asked a somewhat-contentious question, "So, what did you do to Alice Miller?" He was referring to an animosity that Miller apparently held toward me, which I had been confused by myself.

I answered truthfully that I had never met her and had no idea. The only thing that I could think of was that a couple of years before, Joyce had written her regarding my work, thinking that we were both of the same mind regarding human suffering. Joyce had included two of my journal articles. I remembered that Miller had seemed somewhat hostile at the time, emphasizing the importance of her work. I'd been surprised by her reaction, but I soon forgot about the entire incident.

I knew that Ronnie was trying to bait me with his remark, expecting me to be defensive, but I felt relaxed and open. Ignoring my response, he walked out to the balcony once again. But when he returned, he sat down, as if he had come to some sort of decision.

We sat in silence for a few moments. Then, out of curiosity, I asked him, "How do you feel writing in this setting?" Unbeknownst to me, Ronnie was struggling with writer's block. He told me that he was trying to finish a book about love and was completely stuck. We talked about writing, and I noticed that his tension eased. When we spoke of locations for writing, I told him humorously that my creative work largely took place when I was on the toilet, leading to an unusual condition as a side effect. Leaving my testicles hanging in midair for long periods of time eventually led to a habitually painful, aching sensation in my groin, an occupational hazard that could only be corrected by changing my modus operandi.

Ronnie and I, along with Marguerite, Tam, Joyce, and the woman who was Ronnie's client, engaged in dialogue for five solid hours without ever getting up. The night was filled with animated conversation punctuated by the exchange of comical anecdotes. Somehow, Tam ended up telling the story about our visit to the San Francisco Zoo, where there was an impressive gorilla exhibit. Standing outside the enclosure, we were observing the gorillas as they moved about on an island that was surrounded by a deep moat. One dominant male stood out as much larger than the others. Noting his small sex organ relative to his gigantic body, I uttered a derogatory comment. No sooner were the words out of my mouth when the mighty beast stopped what he was doing, stood up, and looked across the crowd, directly at me. Then, as if in response to my insult, he picked up a huge lump of shit, molded it into a tight ball, and hurled it in my direction. It flew over the heads of the other onlookers and hit me directly on the shoulder of my brand-new leather jacket. A moment later, an announcement came over the loudspeaker, warning the crowd not to throw food or other objects into the cages and to respect the animals' rights. I shouted, "What about us? What about us? We have rights, too!"

In addition to the humorous banter, Ronnie and I compared ideas and shared common experiences. We found that there were many amazing coincidences in our lives. For example, we were both mature fathers of two-year-old boys. As I mentioned, my son was named Ronnie, after Laing and a close friend of mine. That evening, he was bundled up, asleep, on the floor near me. Laing's son, Charles, had been put to bed upstairs. Laing described Marguerite as especially protective of their son, and he was amused at the contrast between our casualness and her compulsivity.

Also coincidentally, Laing had visited John Rosen's treatment center in the 1950s, not long after I had finished my internship there. As young therapists, we had both worked for extensive periods with schizophrenic patients and had been unusually attuned to them as people in distress. We felt a mixture of compassion and a sincere interest in their psychotic productions and bizarre behavior. Working with these regressed patients brought out powerful counter-transference reactions of tenderness and parental concern in each of us.

We didn't necessarily have the same approach to psychotherapy, particularly pertaining to the treatment of schizophrenia, but we had a lot in common personally: our experiences, our relationships, and our belief in human rights and individuality. We were both leading unconventional lives, and, even though we had grown up far apart—me in Brooklyn, New York, and Laing in Glasgow, Scotland—there was a lot of overlap.

Ronnie was particularly interested in the dynamics of my group of friends because he was still trying to understand why the Philadelphia Association, his experience of sharing life with friends and associates, had ended up being a disappointment to him. As I described my close friendships and the lifestyle that "our group" had created, he smiled wryly and looked directly into my eyes, saying, "I have a feeling that you must have had something to do with all of this."

As the hours passed, we let our minds soar. Each of us was stimulated by the other. By the time the evening was over, we liked one another immensely and had achieved a rare compatibility. I gave Ronnie the manuscript of my new book, *Compassionate Child-Rearing*, because he had expressed interest in reading my latest theoretical ideas about families and parenting practices.

Considering the peculiar circumstances that had brought us together, in many ways our meeting amounted to a mystical experience. It had a remarkable impact on the patient Ronnie was working with when we arrived. When she joined our party, she appeared confused and disheveled and was definitely hallucinating. But as the evening wore on, she gradually pulled herself together, gathering her hair into a bun and straightening her clothes and, little by little, she joined in the conversation. It was an amazing transformation and, by the end of the evening, she appeared to be quite normal. To tell the truth, I think that we were all transformed.

When Tam, Joyce, and I left Ronnie and Marguerite in the early hours of the morning, there were warm and emotional good-byes; we all felt that we had experienced something extraordinary. There was an exhilarating sense that, from that point forward, Ronnie and I would become increasingly important in one another's lives. It was as though each of us had found the friend we had always longed for. I savored the thought of an ongoing relationship, distinguished by equality and mutual regard. Although both of us were surrounded by loving and admiring associates and friends, in some sense we each felt alone and were badly in need of true companionship.

A few weeks later, Ronnie phoned my office. He had completed reading *Compassionate Child-Rearing* and suggested that he help edit my manuscript. He felt that it was a significant contribution to the field but thought the text needed additional editing in order to have its full impact. He said that the book closely paralleled his own ideas about child rearing. The shared sentiments were so important to him that he offered to meet me in Los Angeles to work on the project. He was happy to learn that I was still on our boat in the Med.

Arrangements were made to meet in the south of France, and Ronnie, along with Marguerite and Charles, rendezvoused with Tam and me, our children, and our group of friends aboard the *Tamara*.

When I greeted Ronnie in Monaco, I felt sad to notice that his health had deteriorated considerably in the month since I had seen him; he was weak and pale and had lost a lot of weight. Nonetheless, he was anxious to begin our project. He and I joined forces and worked feverishly, completely editing the book in a matter of days. Ours was a joyful association; during those sixteen-hour marathons, there were many intellectual exchanges. Ronnie told me that he was getting satisfaction from editing my book because he felt that this was the book on child rearing that he had always wanted to write. While sailing with us, he was completing his own book on love. So much written material was being produced that our printer kept overheating and could only be revived by putting it in the freezer to cool down.

The day after we completed the editing, we celebrated the occasion with Jean-Pierre Soubrier, a French psychiatrist, suicidologist, and close friend of mine, at his country home in le Plan-de-la-Tour. None of us will ever forget the magnificent party that night with the delicious lamb roasted over a pit, the gentle free-flowing affection of close companions, and the remarkable aggregation of talented and interesting individuals. Ronnie and I were like a comedy team as we moved about the gathering. Ronnie was conversing with two elderly English women who were admirers of his psychological and literary accomplishments, and he called me over, "I want you to meet my friend, the Rabbi. He can tell you the answer to your question." He loved to call me by that nickname; it was part of a good-natured routine. I feigned annoyance but enjoyed the repartee. I liked my friend's playful way of bringing me into the serious conversation with the ladies.

Later, Ronnie teased Susan, an old friend of mine, about her fear of the water. Susan could rarely be persuaded to take a dip in the ocean or even a swimming pool. Laing reasoned with her, "Susan, try to drown yourself. See if you can. Jump in the pool and try to drown, Susan. I'll bet you can't do it!" I interjected, "Take the bet; you can't lose, Susan." By then, we had all donned swimsuits; Ronnie had dived into the pool to further encourage her, and she was convinced to chance it. Susan had a delightful time swimming with her newfound friend and ally.

Driving back to the boat after the festivities, we were in the best of spirits. Susan told funny stories about her honeymoon and amusing incidents from the accumulated folklore of our friendship circle. Ronnie and Marguerite were taken with her humor and laughed until they physically hurt. It was a delightful drive through the dark night as we wound our way from the black hills to the sea.

In St. Tropez the next afternoon, less than two months after our chance meeting in Austria, following a set of tennis between us, the brilliant, extraordinary, and lovable man suddenly collapsed and died. The experience had shifted from absolute joy to agony in less than twenty-four hours. Now, years later, when I think about that fatal afternoon, I feel the pain almost as intensely as I did then. I still haven't been able to come to terms with the horrific event that deprived me of the unique and highly valued camaraderie that I had experienced for such a brief time.

Needless to say, I was traumatized by Laing's untimely death. Only a couple of days before, in Nice, I was tossing a baseball around on the dock and Ronnie mentioned that he liked sports and challenged me to a game of tennis. The morning after the party, we heard about a tennis club not far from our boat in St. Tropez. We figured that this was our chance, grabbed our tennis racquets and shoes, and headed over to the courts.

I was immediately apprehensive. It was an extremely hot day, and Ronnie still looked frail to me. I was afraid of him exerting himself. On the courts, I was determined to take it easy, but he played well and was beginning to beat me badly. My competitive feeling was aroused and I tried harder, and it became a close match. Suddenly Ronnie asked for a break. We sat beside the court, and he complained that he was not feeling well.

He apologized for stopping the match and promised a better game next time, but it was obvious that he was in serious trouble. He looked terrible, he was ghastly pale and very weak. With my friends' assistance, I helped him to the van, supporting him in my arms as we walked, his head resting on my shoulder. He lay down across the middle row of seats, and I took the wheel. As I pulled out of the parking lot, I said, "We've got to get him to a doctor!" Ronnie growled, "What kind of doctor?" and those were his last words. He was tossing and turning as my friends tried to comfort him. Finally, he became still.

I remember driving the car through the crowded streets, beating my hands on the steering wheel in a futile attempt to kill the pain. Several of my friends were still holding Ronnie, and everyone in the car was crying loudly as we drove back toward St. Tropez central and found a hospital. Marguerite rushed to meet us there, arriving in a state of shock and disbelief to receive the terrible news. Jean-Pierre came to help her navigate the depressing formalities and to make arrangements to transport Ronnie's body to Scotland for the funeral.

Once we were back on the boat, we delivered the news to all of our friends, many of whom had become his friends, too. I was tormented to inform Natasha and Max that their father was dead. I was so tortured. I decided to take our shore boat out, and I drove along at high speed, bouncing on the waves. In some crazy way, I wanted to embrace life and the living. I felt invigorated by the experience, but at the same time there was no relief from the aching sadness.

Two days later, Tam and I accompanied Laing's family to London and then drove them to Scotland. The final ceremony took place in a cold, Gothic cathedral in Glasgow. Afterward, I returned to my ranch in California, where we began renovation of the landscape. I involved myself in strenuous physical labor in an unconscious effort to shut off the pain. We cut a lot of bricks and laid many pathways as I did my best to process Ronnie's death. Gradually my grief became more intermittent, but it has never gone away.

Sometime later, I was honored to be asked to present my recollections of Ronnie Laing in a memorial service in New York City. I could not attend the conference, so Carl Whitaker read my eulogy.

DEDICATION AND TRIBUTE TO R. D. LAING[1]

My name is Bob Firestone. Ronald Laing and I were the closest of friends at the time of his unfortunate death, and I was present at the end. Let me share with you my sentiments written the following morning, in tears:

> I met R. D. Laing face-to-face for the first time this summer, a chance meeting in Austria; perhaps it was magic. Before that, we were familiar only through our writings and viewing each other as we appeared in documentary films. I found a friend, the hours passed quickly, and I sailed on.
>
> Later I received a call, "I read your book. It is a strong book, an important book, but it needs some work on literary style. I fear that without these stylistic changes, it will fall on even more deaf ears."
>
> My response, "Join me for a sail. Come to Portofino or Nice and we'll talk."
>
> He came and we worked on the book straight through many days and nights. There was a sense of urgency in the work. We shared ideas of all varieties and came to know and love each other. When he first arrived, I noted his frailty and ill health, yet days of sun, and the companionship of other friends and loved ones seemed to help. A light came back into his eyes. He was truly happy at sea. He swam, he socialized, he embraced his children, and he made new friends. In St. Tropez, six days after coming aboard, he died suddenly. And I cried for the loss.
>
> Let me tell you what I know of this man. He was a hurt man, angry in the best sense, strong and stubborn, with an uncanny brilliance. He cared deeply and passionately about people, human rights, and psychological justice. He was uncompromising in his honesty. Tortured by what he saw, there was not much that he didn't see. He was pained by all that was phony, perverse, and cruel. He remained finely tuned to all that was contradictory and paradoxical, exhibiting a wonderful insight and humor about existential issues.

Lastly, he had enormous love and tender feelings for the plight of children. When commenting on Bettelheim's contribution to psychology at the Evolution of Psychotrupy Conference in Phoenix in 1985, tears filled his eyes as he suggested that Bettelheim deserved the Nobel Prize for his work with disturbed children.

Do not forget such a man. He is one in a billion—an original original. Do not be put off by his unconventionality, his unique style of expression and individuality, his personal freedom, his anger and his pain directed against all that is banal and false. He was concerned with injustices that you may not recognize as unjust and may actually embrace. Yet these forces threaten your humanness and personal sense of self, your feeling and being. Although you may be challenged and frightened by this man and his ideas, he is your ultimate ally.

Ronnie was a truly compassionate man. He brought this feeling to the work on my book *Compassionate Child-Rearing*, and there are no words that can do justice to the gratitude I feel.

In the foreword that we were editing, Ronnie wrote, "Firestone is not a preacher. He is a clinician through and through." Then, in a clever play on words so typical of him, he added, "But maybe he should take a chance on preaching what he practices."

In his remark, Laing was referring not only to the parenting practices that I endorsed but also to the lifestyle that my friends and I embrace. He observed that we in the friendship circle base our lives on a policy of being open to all of our feelings, being truthful, and living with integrity. We believe in conducting ourselves according to sound ethical principles of altruism, respect, and concern for others. His statement was an acknowledgement that much of this ideology was based on concepts and values that I had contributed.

In reality, my relationship to this group has not just been that of a contributor; it has been an experience of mutual giving and receiving. I am a person who has benefited greatly from the friend-ship circle. I have profound respect for the intelligence, courage, and honesty of the many people involved, Laing included, and I am deeply indebted to each person for what he or she has contrib-uted to our life together.

HOW TO INCORPORATE
VOICE THERAPY INTO YOUR LIFE

hope that you have enjoyed these stories and that you have gleaned something from them that can prove valuable in your own life. As you saw in the chapters "Demon on My Shoulder," "Regression," and "Daddy's Girl," the application of voice-therapy techniques and concepts changed patients' lives and led to greater happiness. Therefore, I would like to offer more of an understanding of how voice therapy may be of help to you. You might ask yourself, "How can I get to my own voices and understand them, and how would that be useful to me in my development as a person?"

To access your voices, think of times when you have said something stupid or inappropriate and thought to yourself, "I'm such an idiot!" or when you accidentally made a mistake and called yourself a fool. These rather-innocuous voice attacks are only the tip of an iceberg. In my book *Voice Therapy*, I expand on how voices operate.

> A person prepares to give a speech and thinks: "You're going to make a fool of yourself. What if you forget everything you were going to say or act stupid?"
>
> A man calls an attractive woman for a date and hears: "Why should she go out with *you*? Look at you! She probably has lots of better offers."
>
> A man on vacation checks into a high-rise hotel, steps onto his balcony to look at the view and, noting the drop-off, has the crazy thought: "What if you jump?" Feeling anxious, he unconsciously steps back from the ledge.

Mr. X, driving along the freeway, thinks: "Why don't you drive across the center divider or off the side of the road? Why don't you just close your eyes for a minute?" He pictures a tragic accident—images that torment him and make him uneasy.

During sex, Mr. Y thinks: "You're not going to be able to keep your erection," and actually begins to feel cut off from his sexual feelings.

An alcoholic tells himself: "What's the harm in having another drink? You deserve it—you've had a hard day." The next day, in the throes of a hangover, he thinks, "You let everyone down again. You're a despicable person."

In the last moments of life, a suicidal patient thinks: "Go ahead, end it all! Just pull the trigger and it'll all be over."

Thoughts such as these have always concerned me and aroused my curiosity. What were the common threads underlying the apparent attacks on self or self-destructive urges? Why, for example, did the motorist picture himself crashing into the center divider? Were his thoughts and mental images simply part of a self-protective process that was warning him of realistic dangers and potential harm? Were they just meaningless ruminations? Did these thoughts indicate a human propensity for self-hatred?

In studying the manifestations of this thought process, my associates and I have found that this type of thinking is widespread and that a person's actions and general approach to life are regulated or controlled by this manner of thinking. For example, the man in the hotel *did* step back from the ledge, even though he disregarded the command to jump. And Mr. X ignored the urge to drive across the divider, but felt uneasy and depressed following these thoughts and images. Mr. Y *did* have difficulty sexually after running himself down as a man. We observed that even when disregarded or contradicted, this thought process had negative consequences. Psychotherapists have long been aware that people tend to think destructively, that they have many misconceptions of self, or that they have a "shadow" side to their personality.[1]

There are many ways that people can become more aware of their negative thought processes and their anti-self. The anti-self system refers to the accumulation of internalized cynical or hostile voices that represent the defensive aspect of the personality; the "enemy within" that predisposes much of a person's misery and malfunction in life. Voice therapy exposes the split that exists in each person between the real self and the incorporated negative parental attitudes that make up the anti-self.

1. Think of unpleasant thoughts you have about yourself or criticisms you make of your body, your intelligence, your limitations or your personality.
2. Be aware of your mood changes and ask yourself what you were thinking about yourself at the time that your mood changed.
3. Recognize situations that trigger your negative thinking and become aware that you have turned against yourself.
4. Notice when you are thinking people don't like you and examine the thoughts that you are imagining they are having about you.
5. Be wary of any cynical thoughts toward yourself or others; they may be valuable clues of how you are attacking yourself.

After becoming aware of these specific thoughts, change them from the first person to the second person. Imagine saying them aloud to yourself as statements *about* you. Becoming aware of your voice attacks is the first step in helping to free yourself from their negative impact. Putting your self-attacks in the second person separates you from them. This distance allows you to have perspective, which allows for insight. It is valuable to try to understand where your negative thoughts originated. How did you come to feel badly toward yourself? Which incidents in your life may have led to this type of destructive thinking?

Uncovering the way you attack yourself allows you to identify the source of much of your unnecessary suffering and offers the possibility of real change. It also helps you to understand that your unpleasant moods, bad decisions, and negative actions are often the result of self-destructive attacks. And finally, it suggests new directions to take to counter your voices. As noted in the introduction, in voice therapy, therapist and client collaborate in formulating constructive thoughts and behaviors that go against the voice, and these expand the world for the person and open up new possibilities. For example, a shy, inward woman who was afraid to apply for a job because her voices told her she would never qualify took a chance and acted on the corrective suggestion to give it a try—and to her surprise she was hired. Although the ideas above pertain primarily to psychotherapy, to a certain extent you can actively apply the voice concept to yourself and make basic changes.

It is valuable to scrutinize your negative thoughts to determine whether there is any truth to your attacks. However, even when aspects of your self-attacks are true, there is no need to approach the matter in a hostile manner. Instead, you can work on changing any actual negative characteristics that you discover. It serves no worthwhile purpose to attack yourself; it just leaves you feeling bad. On the other hand, simply working on changing undesirable traits can contribute to significant changes that improve your life. To a large extent, you have the power to develop and, in fact, to re-create yourself to become a person whom you admire. Although there is always anxiety as people grow, it is worthwhile to struggle through it to come out on the other end.

You can achieve this by striving to live up to your own values and priorities in life. And if there are failures along the way, you can have compassion for yourself and increase your efforts toward changing rather than attacking yourself. I cannot emphasize enough the importance of liking and appreciating yourself. As you approach this goal, you will find a sense of inner harmony because, above all, you need to respect the person you are to feel good in life.

The dilemma faced by people who have progressed and developed in psychotherapy is essentially no different from that faced by every human being. The alternatives are clear: without challenging destructive aspects of yourself as represented by the voice, you will gradually submit to an alien, hostile point of view and shut down your authentic self and unique outlook.

In conclusion, there is no hidden significance to life to be discovered; we must each find our own personal meaning. It is only the investment of ourselves as individuals—in our feelings, our creativity, our interests, and our personal choice of people and activities—that is special. Indeed, we imbue experiences with meaning through our own spirit rather than the opposite, and our priorities express our true identity.

The ultimate goal of my therapy is to help clients move away from compulsive, self-limiting lifestyles so that they can expand their lives and tolerate more gratification in reality. We hope to help individuals achieve a free and independent existence, remain open to experience and feelings, and maintain the ability to respond appropriately to both positive and negative events in their lives. To this end, the process of identifying the "voice" and the associated feelings of self-hatred and rage toward oneself, combined with corrective strategies of behavioral change, significantly expand the client's boundaries and bring about a more positive sense of self.

NOTES AND REFERENCES

FOREWORD

Carlson, E. A. 1998. "A Prospective Longitudinal Study of Disorganized Attachment and Psychiatric Relapse: A Meta-Analysis." *Archives of General Psychiatry* 55:547–52.

Cyr, C., E. M. Euser, M. J. Bakermans-Kranenburg, and M. H. van Ijzendoorn. 2010. "Attachment Security and Disorganization in Maltreating and High-Risk Families: A Series of Meta-Analyses." *Development and Psychopathology* 22, no. 1:87–108.

Lyons-Ruth, K., and D. Jacobvitz. 2008. "Attachment Disorganization: Genetic Factors, Parenting Contexts, and Developmental Transformation from Infancy to Adulthood." In *Handbook of Attachment: Theory, Research, and Clinical Applications*, edited by J. Cassidy and P. R. Shaver, 666–97. 2nd ed. New York: Guilford.

Lyons-Ruth, K., C. Yellin, S. Melnick, and G. Atwood. 2005. "Expanding the Concept of Unresolved Mental States: Hostile/Helpless States of Mind on the Adult Attachment Interview are Associated with Disrupted Mother–Infant Communication and Infant Disorganization." *Development and Psychopathology* 17:1–23.

MacDonald, H. Z., M. Beeghly, W. Grant-Knight, M. Augustyn, R. W. Woods, H. Cabral, et al. 2008. "Longitudinal Association between Infant Disorganized Attachment and Childhood Posttraumatic Stress Symptoms." *Development and Psychopathology* 20, no. 2:493–508.

Mackenzie, C. 2009. "Personal Identity, Narrative Integration, and Embodiment." In *Embodiment and Agency*, edited by S. Campbell, L. Meynell, and S. Sherwin, 100–25. University Park: Pennsylvania State University Press.

Madigan, S., M. J. Bakermans-Kranenburg, M. H. Van Ijzendoorn, G. Moran, D. R. Pederson, and D. Benoit. 2006. "Unresolved States of Mind, Anomalous Parental Behavior, and Disorganized Attachment: A Review and Meta-Analysis of a Transmission Gap." *Attachment & Human Development* 8, no. 2:89–111.

Madigan, S., G. Moran, C. Schuengel, D. R. Pederson, and R. Otten. 2007. "Unresolved Maternal Attachment Representations, Disrupted Maternal Behavior and Disorganized Attachment in Infancy: Links to Toddler Behavior Problems." *Journal of Child Psychology and Psychiatry* 48, no. 10:1042–50.

Siegel, D. J. 2012. *The Developing Mind: How Relationships and the Brain Interact to Shape Who We Are*. New York: Guilford.

Teicher, M. H., A. Tomoda, and S. L. Andersen. 2006. "Neurobiological Consequences of Early Stress and Childhood Maltreatment: Are Results from Human and Animal Studies Comparable?" *Annals of the New York Academy of Sciences* 1071:313–23.

Teicher, M. H. 2007. "The Role of Experience in Brain Development: Adverse Effects of Childhood Maltreatment." In *Mind, Brain, and Education in Reading Disorders*, edited by K. W. Fischer, J. H. Bernstein, and M. H. Immordino-Yang, 176–77. Cambridge: Cambridge University Press.

Vygotsky, L. S. 1986. *Thought and Language*. Edited by A. Kozulin. Cambridge, MA: MIT Press.

Weinfield, N. S., G. J. Whaley, and B. Egeland. 2004. "Continuity, Discontinuity, and Coherence in Attachment from Infancy to Late Adolescence: Sequelae of Organization and Disorganization." *Attachment & Human Development* 6, no. 1:73–97.

Zhang, T., and M. Meaney. 2010. "Epigenetics and the Environmental Regulation of the Genome and Its Function." *Annual Review of Psychology* 61:439–66.

INTRODUCTION

1. Regarding the therapeutic relationship and personal qualities of the therapist, see the research summary on the therapeutic relationship and psychotherapy outcome in Michael J. Lambert and Dean E. Barley, *Psychotherapy: Theory, Research, Practice, Training* 38, no. 4 (2001): 357–61, http://dx.doi.org/10.1037/0033-3204.38.4.357. "Common factors such as empathy, warmth, and the therapeutic relationship have been shown to correlate more highly with client outcome than specialized treatment interventions" (ibid., abstract).

CHAPTER 5: DANCE OF DEATH

1. Robert W. Firestone, "Voice Therapy," in *What Is Psychotherapy? Contemporary Perspectives*, edited by J. Zeig and W. Munion (San Francisco: Jossey-Bass, 1990), pp. 68–74.

CHAPTER 6: CONTROL

1. Robert W. Firestone and Joyce Catlett, *The Ethics of Interpersonal Relationships* (London: Karnac Books, 2009), p. 54.

CHAPTER 7: THERAPIST OR TYRANT?

1. John N. Rosen, *Direct Analysis* (New York: Grune & Stratton, 1953).

2. Honor Whiteman, "Schizophrenia Breakthrough: Scientists Shed Light on Biological Cause," *Medical News Today*, February 4, 2016, http://www.medicalnewstoday

.com/articles/306063.php (accessed August 18, 2016); and Filippo Varese et al., "Childhood Adversities Increase the Risk of Psychosis: A Meta-Analysis of Patient-Control, Prospective- and Cross-Sectional Cohort Studies," *Schizophrenia Bulletin*, February 27, 2012, http://schizophreniabulletin.oxfordjournals.org/content/38/4/661.full (accessed August 18, 2016).

CHAPTER 8: REGRESSION

1. See R. W. Firestone, "The 'Inner Voice' and Suicide," *Psychotherapy* 23, no. 3 (1986): 439–47; R. W. Firestone and L. Firestone, "Suicide Reduction and Prevention," in *What's the Good of Counseling & Psychotherapy?* edited by C. Feltham (London: Sage Publications, 2002), pp. 48–80; R. W. Firestone and R. H. Seiden, "Suicide and the Continuum of Self-Destructive Behavior," *Journal of American College Health* 38, no. 5 (1990): 207–13; and R. A. Heckler, *Waking Up, Alive: The Descent, the Suicide Attempt, and the Return to Life* (New York: Ballantine, 1994).

CHAPTER 11: DADDY'S GIRL

1. The article was adapted for Robert W. Firestone and Lisa Firestone, "Methods for Overcoming the Fear of Intimacy," chap. 21 in *The Handbook of Closeness and Intimacy*, edited by D. Mashek and A. Aron (Mahwah, NJ: Lawrence Erlbaum, 2004). Also see Robert W. Firestone and Joyce Catlett, "Why Relationships Fail," chap. 2 in *Fear of Intimacy* (Washington, DC: American Psychological Association Books, 1999).

AFTERWORD: R. D. LAING AND THE DIVIDED SELF

1. Parts of this eulogy were reprinted from "Tribute to R. D. Laing" in *Compassionate Child-Rearing: An In-Depth Approach to Optimal Parenting* (Santa Barbara, CA: Glendon Association, 1990), pp. v–vi.

APPENDIX: HOW TO INCORPORATE VOICE THERAPY INTO YOUR LIFE

1. Robert W. Firestone, *Voice Therapy: A Psychotherapeutic Approach to Self-Destructive Behavior* (Santa Barbara, CA: Glendon Association, 1988), pp. 31–33.

SELECT BIBLIOGRAPHY

Please note that the references are listed chronologically rather than alphabetically, to reflect the development of the author's theory and methodology from 1957 to the present. References for Lisa Firestone, PhD, are also listed chronologically.

Alper, G. *Paranoia of Everyday Life: Escaping the Enemy Within*. Amherst, NY: Prometheus Books, 2005.

Bassett, J. F. "Psychological Defenses against Death Anxiety: Integrating Terror Management Theory and Firestone's Separation Theory." *Death Studies* 31 (2007): 727–50.

Beck, J. S. *Cognitive Therapy: Basics and Beyond*. New York: Guilford, 1995.

Becker, E. *The Denial of Death*. New York: Free Press, 1997. (Original work, 1973.)

Breggin, P. R. *Guilt, Shame, and Anxiety: Understanding and Overcoming Negative Emotions*. Amherst, NY: Prometheus Books, 2014.

Cozolino, L. *Why Therapy Works: Using Our Minds to Change Our Brains*. New York: W. W. Norton, 2015.

De Zulueta, F. *From Pain to Violence: The Traumatic Roots of Destructiveness*. London: Whurr Publishers, 1993.

Doucette-Gates, A., R. W. Firestone, and L. Firestone. "Assessing Violent Thoughts: The Relationship between Thought Processes and Violent Behavior." *Psychologica Belgica* 39, no. 2/3 (1999): 113–34.

Eckhardt, C. I., and J. Schram. "Cognitive Behavioral Interventions for Partner-Abusive Men." In *Strengths-Based Batterer Intervention: A New Paradigm in Ending Family Violence*, edited by Peter Lehmann and Catherine A Simmons. New York: Springer Publishing Company, 2009. (Kindle edition.)

Ellis, A. *Overcoming Destructive Beliefs, Feelings, and Behaviors: New Directions for Rational Emotive Behavioral Therapy*. Amherst, NY: Prometheus Books, 2001.

Fierman, L. B., ed. *Effective Psychotherapy: The Contribution of Hellmuth Kaiser*. New York: Free Press, 1965.

Firestone, L. "The Firestone Voice Scale for Self-Destructive Behavior: Investigating the Scale's Validity and Reliability." PhD diss., California School of Professional Psychology, Los Angeles. *Dissertation Abstracts International* 52, no. 3338B (1991).

———. "Assessment and Management of the Suicidal Client." *Los Angeles Psychologist* 10, no. 5 (1991).

————. "Assessment and Management of the Suicidal Client—Part II: Developing Treatment Plan for the Client at Risk." *Los Angeles Psychologist* 11, no. 7 (1996).

————. "Separation Theory and Voice Therapy Methodology Applied to the Treatment of Katie: A Diary-Based Retrospective Case Conceptualization and Treatment Approach." In *Katie's Diary: Unlocking the Mystery of a Suicide*, edited by D. Lester. New York and Hove: Brunner Routledge, 2004, pp. 161–88.

————. "Voice Therapy: A Treatment for Depression and Suicide." In *Assessment, Treatment, and Prevention of Suicidal Behavior*, edited by R. Yufit and D. Lester. New York: John Wiley, 2004, pp. 235–77.

————. "Suicide and the Inner Voice." In *Cognition and Suicide: Theory, Research and Practice*, edited by T. Ellis. Washington, DC: American Psychological Association, 2006, pp. 119–47.

————. "The Critical Inner Voice That Drives Suicide." In *Suicide in the Words of Suicidologists*, edited by M. Pompili. Hauppage, NY: Nova Science, 2010.

————. "Rethinking Dexter." In *The Psychology of Dexter*, edited by B. DePaulo. Dallas, TX: SmartPop Books, 2010, pp. 17–32.

————. "Separation Theory and Voice Therapy Methodology." In *The Social Psychology of Meaning, Mortality and Choice*, edited by P. R. Shaver and M. Mikulincer. Washington, DC: American Psychological Association, 2011.

Firestone, L., and J. Catlett. "The Treatment of Sylvia Plath." *Death Studies* 22 (1998): 667–92.

Firestone, R. W. "A Concept of the Schizophrenic Process." Unpublished PhD diss., University of Denver, 1957.

————. *The Fantasy Bond: Structure of Psychological Defenses*. Santa Barbara, CA: Glendon Association, 1985.

————. *Voice Therapy: A Psychotherapeutic Approach to Self-Destructive Behavior*. Santa Barbara, CA: Glendon Association, 1988.

————. "Parenting Groups Based on Voice Therapy." *Psychotherapy* 26, no. 4 (1989): 524–29.

————. *Compassionate Child-Rearing: An In-Depth Approach to Optimal Parenting*. Santa Barbara, CA: Glendon Association, 1990.

————. "Voice Therapy." In *What Is Psychotherapy? Contemporary Perspectives*, edited by J. Zeig and W. Munion. San Francisco: Jossey-Bass, 1990.

————. "Prescription for Psychotherapy." *Psychotherapy* 27, no. 4 (1990): 627–35.

————. "Voices during Sex: Application of Voice Therapy to Sexuality." *Journal of Sex and Marital Therapy* 16, no. 4 (1990): 258–74.

————. "A New Perspective on the Oedipal Complex: A Voice Therapy Session." *Psychotherapy* 31 (1994): 342–51.

————. "Psychological Defenses against Death Anxiety." In *Death Anxiety Handbook: Research, Instrumentation, and Application*, edited by R. A. Neimeyer. Washington, DC: Taylor & Francis, 1994.

———. "The Origins of Ethnic Strife." *Mind and Human Interaction* 7 (1996): 167–80.

———. *Combating Destructive Thought Processes: Voice Therapy and Separation Theory.* Thousand Oaks, CA: Sage, 1997.

———. *Suicide and the Inner Voice: Risk Assessment, Treatment, and Case Management.* Thousand Oaks, CA: Sage, 1997.

———. "Voice Therapy." In *Favorite Counseling and Therapy Techniques: 51 Therapists Share Their Most Creative Strategies*, edited by H. G. Rosenthal. Washington, DC: Accelerated Development, 1998.

———. "The Death of Psychoanalysis and Depth Therapy." *Psychotherapy: Theory/Research/Practice/Training* 39, no. 3 (2002): 223–32.

———. "The Ultimate Resistance." *Journal of Humanistic Psychology* 55, no. 1: 77–101, http://jhp.sagepub.com/content/early/2014/03/20/0022167814527166(2015).

Firestone, R. W., and Joyce Catlett, *Psychological Defenses in Everyday Life*. Santa Barbara, CA: Glendon Association, 1989. (Originally published as *The Truth: A Psychological Cure*. New York: MacMillan Publishing, 1981.)

———. *Fear of Intimacy*. Washington, DC: American Psychological Association, 1999.

———. *Beyond Death Anxiety: Achieving Life-Affirming Death Awareness*. New York: Springer Publishing, 2009.

———. *The Ethics of Interpersonal Relationships*. London: Karnac Books, 2009.

Firestone, R. W., and L. Firestone. "Voices in Suicide: The Relationship between Self-Destructive Thought Processes, Maladaptive Behavior, and Self-Destructive Manifestations." *Death Studies* 22, no. 5 (1998): 411–43.

———. "Suicide Reduction and Prevention." In *What's the Good of Counseling & Psychotherapy?* edited by C. Feltham. London: Sage Publications, 2002.

———. "Methods for Overcoming the Fear of Intimacy." In *The Handbook of Closeness and Intimacy*, edited by D. Mashek and A. Aron. Mahwah, NJ: Lawrence Erlbaum, 2004.

———. "Separation Theory and Voice Therapy Methodology." In *The Social Psychology of Meaning, Mortality, and Choice*, edited by P. R. Shaver and M. Mikulincer. Washington, DC: American Psychological Association, 2012.

Firestone, R. W., Lisa Firestone, and Joyce Catlett. *Conquer Your Critical Inner Voice: A Revolutionary Program to Counter Negative Thoughts and Live Free from Imagined Limitations*. Oakland, CA: New Harbinger Publications, 2002.

———. *Creating a Life of Meaning and Compassion: The Wisdom of Psychotherapy.* Washington, DC: American Psychological Association, 2003.

———. *Sex and Love in Intimate Relationships*. Washington, DC: American Psychological Association, 2006.

———. *The Self under Siege: A Therapeutic Model of Differentiation*. New York: Routledge, 2013.

Fonagy, P., et al. *Affect Regulation, Mentalization, and the Development of the Self*. New York: Other Press, 2002.

Freud, A. *The Ego and the Mechanisms of Defense*. Rev. ed. Madison, CT: International Universities Press, 1966.

Garbarino, J. *Lost Boys: Why Our Sons Turn Violent and How We Can Save Them*. New York: Free Press: Anchor Books, 1999.

———. *Listening to Killers: Lessons Learned from My Twenty Years as a Psychological Expert Witness in Murder Cases*. Oakland: University of California Press, 2015.

Gilligan, J. *Preventing Violence*. New York: Thames & Hudson, 2001.

Goldberg, C. *The Evil We Do: The Psychoanalysis of Destructive People*. Amherst, NY: Prometheus Books, 2000.

Greenberg, J. (Hannah Green). *I Never Promised You a Rose Garden*. New York: St Martin's, 1964, 2004.

Greenberg, L. S. *Emotion-Focused Therapy: Coaching Clients to Work through Their Feelings*. Washington, DC: American Psychological Association, 2015.

Karon, B. P., and Gary VandenBos. *Psychotherapy of Schizophrenia: The Treatment of Choice*. Lanham, MD: Rowman & Littlefield, 1981.

Kerr, M. E., and Murray Bowen. *Family Evaluation: An Approach Based on Bowen Theory*. New York: W. W. Norton, 1988.

Kottler, J. A., and Jon Carlson. *The Mummy at the Dining Room Table: Eminent Therapists Reveal Their Most Unusual Cases and What They Teach Us about Human Behavior*. San Francisco: Jossey-Bass, 2003.

———. *On Being a Master Therapist: Practicing What You Preach*. Hoboken, NJ: John Wiley & Sons, 2014.

Laing, R. D. *The Divided Self: An Existential Study in Sanity and Madness*. Middlesex, England: Penguin Books, 1965. (Originally published 1960.)

McKay, M., et al. *The Dialectical Behavior Therapy Skills Workbook; Practical DBT Exercises for Learning Mindfulness, Emotion Regulation & Distress Tolerance*. 1st ed. New Harbinger Self-Help Workbook. Oakland, CA: New Harbinger Publications, 2007.

Mikulincer, M., and Phillip Shaver. *Attachment in Adulthood: Structure, Dynamics, and Change*. New York: Guilford, 2007.

Miller, A. *The Truth Will Set You Free: Overcoming Emotional Blindness and Finding Your True Adult Self*. Translated by Andrew Jenkins. New York: Basic Books, 2001.

Oaklander, V. *Windows to Our Children: A Gestalt Therapy Approach to Children and Adolescents*. Moab, UT: Real People, 1978.

———. *Hidden Treasure: A Map of the Child's Inner Self*. London: Karnac Books, 2006.

Orbach, I. "Existentialism and Suicide." In *Existential and Spiritual Issues in Death Attitudes*, edited by A. Tomer, G. T. Eliason, and P. T. P. Wong. New York: Lawrence Erlbaum, 2008.

Poulter, S. B. *The Father Factor; How Your Father's Legacy Impacts Your Career*. Amherst, NY: Prometheus Books, 2006.

———. *The Mother Factor: How Your Mother's Emotional Legacy Impacts Your Life*. Amherst, NY: Prometheus Books, 2008.

Rosen, J. N. *Direct Analysis*. New York: Grune and Stratton, 1953.

Rosenthal, H. " An Interview with Robert and Lisa Firestone." In *Therapy's Best: Practical*

Advice and Gems of Wisdom from Twenty Accomplished Counselors and Therapists. Binghamton, NY: Haworth, 2006.

Rubin, L *The Man with the Beautiful Voice and More Stories from the Other Side of the Couch.* Boston: Beacon, 2003.

Schneider, K. J. *The Polarized Mind: Why It's Killing Us and What We Can Do about It.* Colorado Springs: University Professors Press, 2013.

Seiden, R. H. "Salutary Effects of Maternal Separation." *Social Work* 10, no. 4 (1965): 25–29.

Siegel, D. J. *Brainstorm: The Power and Purpose of the Teenage Brain.* New York: TarcherPerigee, 2014.

———. *Pocket Guide to Interpersonal Neurobiology: An Integrative Handbook of the Mind.* New York: W. W. Norton, 2012.

Skowron, E. A., and Thomas Schmitt. "Assessing Interpersonal Fusion: Reliability and Validity of a New DSI Fusion with Others Subscale." *Journal of Marital and Family Therapy* 29 (2003): 209–22.

Solomon, S., et al. *The Worm at the Core: On the Role of Death in Life.* New York: Random House, 2015.

Welldon, E. V. *Playing with Dynamite: A Personal Approach to the Psychoanalytic Understanding of Perversions, Violence, and Criminality.* London: Karnac Books, 2011.

Wenzel, A., and A. T. Beck. "A Cognitive Model of Suicidal Behavior: Theory and Treatment." *Applied and Preventive Psychology* 12, no. 4 (2008): 189–201.

Winnicott, D. W. *Home Is Where We Start From: Essays by a Psychoanalyst.* New York: W. W. Norton, 1986.

Yalom, I. *The Gift of Therapy: An Open Letter to a New Generation of Therapists and Their Patients.* New York: HarperCollins Publishers, 2002.

RESOURCES

WEBSITES

A book-specific website, tentatively titled "The Works of Robert Firestone" is under construction and will be launched in October 2016. The site will feature reviews, endorsements, comments, and interviews about *Overcoming the Destructive Inner Voice*, as well as descriptions of the book, the author's profile, photographs, and graphics. Also included are articles and blogs by the author regarding topics addressed in the book. Clips from Glendon Association's extensive archival library of videotaped interviews with Dr. Firestone will gradually be uploaded to the site.

Glendon.org

The Glendon Association is a nonprofit organization committed to saving lives and enhancing mental health by addressing the social problems of suicide, violence, child abuse, and troubled interpersonal relationships. In-depth discussions of our major areas of interest are found in the books and contributed book chapters, articles, and award-winning video documentaries featured on the website.

PsychAlive.com

This is a website created by Glendon to bring psychological information to the general public. The articles, blogs, videos, and workshops featured on PsychAlive introduce visitors to sound psychological principles and practices, while offering an insightful means of coping with life's everyday problems. Articles and blogs written by Dr. Robert Firestone are prominently featured.

PsychAlive also has a YouTube channel, http: //www.psychalive .org/psychalives-youtube-channel/s, which (to date) includes thirty video-clip interviews with Dr. Firestone describing the fantasy bond, the critical inner voice, voice therapy, couple relationships, child rearing, and existential issues.

In 2015, PsychAlive recorded 2,385,000 unique visitors and over four million page views.

RWFirestoneArt.com/

This site features the art of Dr. Robert Firestone, and reviews are also accessible here.

ASSESSMENT INSTRUMENTS

The Glendon Association, in conjunction with Drs. Robert and Lisa Firestone, has produced several valuable screening instruments for self-destructive thoughts and behaviors, as well as for violence and suicide risk. The scales, the Firestone Assessment of Self-Destructive Thoughts (FAST), the Firestone Assessment of Suicide Intent (FASI) and the Firestone Assessment of Violent Intent (FAVI), are published by Psychological Assessment Resources (PAR).

Manuals for Assessment Instruments

FAST: Firestone Assessment of Self-Destructive Thoughts

FAST can be given in an interview format or on paper in fifteen minutes. It is designed for clients aged sixteen or older.

FAVT: Firestone Assessment of Violent Thoughts for Adults

The FAVT can be given in an interview format or on paper in fifteen minutes. It is designed for adults. FAVT items are organized into five levels (i.e., paranoid/suspicious, persecuted misfit, self-depreciating/pseudo-independent, self-aggrandizing, overtly aggressive) and two theoretical subscales (i.e., instrumental/proactive violence, hostile/reactive violence).

FAVT: Firestone Assessment of Violent Thoughts for Adolescents

The FAVT-A is designed to be a brief, efficient indicator of an individual's violence potential. Based on the adult version of the FAVT, this thirty-five-item self-report assesses the underlying thoughts that predispose violent behavior in individuals ages eleven to eighteen years.

References for Assessment Manuals

Firestone, R. W., and L. Firestone. (2006). *Firestone Assessment of Self-Destructive Thoughts (FAST) Manual.* Lutz, FL: Psychological Assessment Resources.
———. (2008a). *Firestone Assessment of Violent Thoughts (FAVT) Manual.* Lutz, FL: Psychological Assessment Resources.
———. (2008b). *Firestone Assessment of Violent Thoughts—Adolescent (FAVT-A) Manual.* Lutz, FL: Psychological Assessment Resources.

DOCUMENTARY FILMS

(The following are distributed through the Glendon Association and to mental-health professionals through www.psychotherapy.net.)

1984. *Voice Therapy with Dr. Robert Firestone.* This film received an honorable mention at the American Film Festival. [40 minutes]

1984. *Teaching Our Children about Feelings.* This video features a lively discussion between several young teenagers and Dr. Robert Firestone about the importance of being in touch with one's feelings. [38 minutes]

1985. *The Fantasy Bond Film Supplement.* [58 Minutes]

1985. *The Inner Voice in Suicide.* This film was a winner at the American Film Festival. In this interview, a young woman recalls events leading up to her serious attempt at suicide. [32 minutes]

1986. *Closeness without Bonds.* This features a moving story of men and women struggling to recapture the essence of their closest, most intimate relationships, set against the background of skillful psychotherapeutic intervention. [38 minutes]

1986. *The Inner Voice in Child Abuse.* This film won the Chris Plaque Award at the Columbus Film Festival. It was presented by James Garbarino at the International Conference on Prevention of Child Abuse. [47 minutes]

1987. *Teenagers Talk about Suicide.* This documentary shows a conversation between Dr. Robert Firestone and several teenagers from a nonclinical population concerning their views of adolescent suicide. [35 minutes]

1987. *Parental Ambivalence.* [34 minutes]

1987. *Hunger versus Love.* In this program, Dr. Robert Firestone clarifies the distinction between parental behavior that leads to an anxious attachment in children and behavior that promotes a secure attachment. [37 minutes]

1988. *The Implicit Pain of Sensitive Child-Rearing.* This film received an honorable mention at the National Council on Family Relations Media Awards. It examines the reasons why many parents find it difficult to sustain loving relationships with, and offer nurturance to, their children, and it clearly reveals the therapeutic process in a parents' group where parents talk about this phenomenon. [43 minutes]

1989. *Of Business and Friendship.* This film earned a certificate of creative excellence at the US Industrial Film and Video Festival. Areas covered by this program include dealing effectively and productively with highly competitive situations among employees; understanding negative reactions to success; and the potential value of the role of a clinical psychologist in a corporate structure. [44 minutes]

1990. *Sex and Marriage.* In this film, participants share personal stories concerning their sexual history in the accepting atmosphere of a couples' group. [43 minutes]

1990. *Sex and Society.* This film won at the National Council on Family Relations Media Awards. It reveals distorted attitudes toward sex and prejudicial views of men and women that are often learned in the family and reinforced by society. [55 minutes]

1990. *Voices in Sex.* This film illustrates the steps in the therapeutic process that can interrupt destructive thought processes experienced by each partner and bring couples back to real feeling. [58 minutes]

1990. *Life, Death & Denial.* This was filmed during a series of seminars on the subject of death anxiety.

1990. *Defenses against Death Anxiety.* This program illustrates the primary dimensions of each person's existential dilemma, revealing how an awareness of one's finite existence can make life and living even more precious.

1991. *Sonya—An Individual Voice Therapy Session.* This film provides an excellent demonstration of voice-therapy methodology. [26 minutes]

1991. *Robert W. Firestone: A Unique Perspective: Parts 1 and 2.* This film features an interview and group discussion with Dr. Firestone regarding his ideas, values, and philosophy of life, and how he developed his theoretical concepts and methodology.

1992. *Voice Therapy: A New Perspective on the Oedipal Complex.* This videotaped session involves a young man who incorporated his father's aggression and jealous rage toward him in the form of self-destructive and suicidal thoughts. [54 minutes]

1993. *Children of the Summer.* This film shares the story of twenty-two young children on a voyage from California to Alaska. It is recommended for parent education groups, elementary and junior-high school audiences, and educators; and it was broadcast nationally on PBS. [58 minutes]

1994. *Invisible Child Abuse.* This film sheds light on patterns of emotional child abuse; it was broadcast nationally on PBS. [49 minutes]

1995. *Inwardness—A Retreat from Feeling.* This film explores the dimensions of an inward, self-parenting lifestyle and methods for challenging destructive modes of thinking. [70 minutes]

1995. *Voices about Relationships.* This film was the winner at the Western Psychological Association Film Festival and earned a certificate of merit. It exposes the key issues within couples that interfere with each partner's ability to relate closely. [46 minutes]

1997. *Exploring Relationships.* In this documentary, participants candidly discuss topics of mate selection, honesty and deception, and the process of learning how to love. [52 minutes]

1997. *Fear of Intimacy—An Examination of Withholding Behavior Patterns.* This is a deeply moving program that explores the barriers to intimacy and closeness. [52 minutes]

1999. *Coping with the Fear of Intimacy.* In this film, four couples participate in an ongoing discussion group and use voice-therapy techniques to identify negative thoughts that interfere with their ability to relate closely. [60 minutes]

2002. *Friendship: A Life of Meaning and Compassion.* This film was a finalist in the New York International Film and Video Competition. Viewers will identify with the moving, personal, and forthright stories of people who talk about their struggles to find personal meaning in life, to achieve success in their careers, and to enrich their family life. [56 minutes]

2005. *Sex, Love, and Intimate Relationships.* This compelling film explores two fundamental questions: "What is healthy sexuality?" and "What is love?" The documentary describes early childhood experiences and societal influences that impact an individual's emerging sexuality.

2008. *Voices of Suicide: Learning from Those Who Lived.* This documentary explores what was going on in the minds of three people who narrowly survived highly lethal suicide attempts. Their accounts, in conjunction with interviews from renowned experts, including Drs. Alan Schore, Israel Orbach, David Jobes, David Rudd, Robert Firestone, and Lisa Firestone, provide valuable insight into the relationship between early developmental experiences and later suicidal behavior. [62 minutes]

2008. *Understanding and Preventing Suicide.* How can you know if your family member or friend may be suicidal? How do you recognize the warning signs? How can you help? Learn from experts in suicide prevention and treatment by watching this video. [28 minutes]

2010. *Voices of Violence: Part 1: The Roots of Violence.* This film reveals the triggers that led several individuals to commit violence, and it identifies the destructive thoughts or "voices" that were directing their behavior. It features interviews with experts in neuroscience and attachment Daniel Siegel, Felicity de Zulueta, David Jones, Peter Fonagy, Donald Meichenbaum, and James Gilligan. The film interweaves these perspectives with the work of Dr. Robert Firestone, which further illuminates the underlying dynamics operating in the mind of violent individuals. [60 minutes]

2011. *Voices of Violence: Part 2: Effective Treatment for Violent Individuals.* This film integrates the narratives of violent individuals participating in two innovative treatment programs, one in San Francisco and the other in Oxford, UK, with interviews of therapists and experts in the field of violence. [56 minutes]

INDEX